Men come in all shapes, sizes, colours and creeds!

They can be infuriating, argumentative, stubborn, unfaithful, egotistical, power-hungry, aggressive, selfish, noisy, restless, pompous, boring, unreasonable, irritating, sullen, unpunctual, greedy, lazy, cheeky, but – somehow – IRRESISTIBLE!

Throughout my life I have spent a great deal of my time MANWATCHING, to quote the title of my schoolday boyfriend, Dr Desmond Morris's, book. So it seemed like a good idea to write about my own experiences in order that other women could play the game too!

Of course, females also fall into many of the categories within these pages, and males are perfectly entitled to answer back or criticize if they choose. But basically it is a light-hearted book for women who are forced to live in what I consider to be very definitely a *man's world* (no matter how much the opposite sex argues that it is the other way around).

Diana Dors

# Diana Dors'
# A–Z of Men

Futura
Macdonald & Co
London & Sydney

A Futura Book

First published in Great Britain in 1984 by Futura
Publications, a Division of Macdonald & Co
(Publishers) Ltd, London & Sydney

ISBN 0 7088 2345 9

Typeset, printed and bound in Great Britain by
Hazell Watson & Viney Limited,
Member of the BPCC Group,
Aylesbury, Bucks

Futura Publications
A Division of
Macdonald & Co (Publishers) Ltd
Maxwell House
74 Worship Street
London EC2A 2EN
A BPCC plc Company

# Preface

Men come in all shapes, sizes, colours and creeds!

They can be infuriating, argumentative, stubborn, unfaithful, egotistical, power-hungry, aggressive, selfish, noisy, restless, pompous, boring, unreasonable, irritating, sullen, unpunctual, greedy, lazy, cheeky, but – somehow – IRRESISTIBLE!

Throughout my life I have spent a great deal of my time MANWATCHING, to quote the title of my schoolday boyfriend, Dr Desmond Morris's, book. So it seemed like a good idea to write about my own experiences in order that other women could play the game too!

Of course, females also fall into many of the categories within these pages, and males are perfectly entitled to answer back or criticize if they choose. But basically it is a light-hearted book for women who are forced to live in what I consider to be very definitely a *man's world* (no matter how much the opposite sex argues that it is the other way around).

Naturally, not all sorts of men are dealt with here, and hopefully most women will never have experienced or need to cope with some of the types described.

But the lucky ones, and certainly the innocent ones, may benefit from reading the results of my findings.

The rest, apart from being amused, might well agree with me that despite the so-called equality of the sexes today, men have had – since the beginning of time – the cards dealt in their favour all the way.

To illustrate my point, a husband can stay out half the night, fall through the door at 5 a.m. (having consumed too much liquor), mutter the old excuse of 'being out with the boys' (regardless of the lipstick on his collar or love bites on his neck), AND fully expect his wife to accept it, even if there is an almighty row!

But if the positions were reversed, imagine the full-scale war *her* behaviour would start! It could culminate in murder or at the very least divorce!

I am not suggesting that we females are perfect in every respect, though frankly I could never envisage us doing some of the things that men do, especially in the extreme areas of perversion or rape.

Perhaps it is because we were put on this earth to give birth, and help create life, rather than take it away or abuse it as many men do to satisfy such motives as greed for power.

Whilst I uphold women's rights in every field, I must add that I am disturbed by the way some women demand to be treated like men, and I have been involved in heated battles with a few of the more masculine-inclined on this point. I do not have much to say in favour of men in this book, but on this I must stick to my guns and also state that there is a limit to which women should be encouraged to invade the sanctity of the 'man's world' – namely in clubs or even public houses, where I honestly feel that both male and female ought to be given the opportunity to enjoy separate relaxation.

Women wishing to be treated as women (and with respect by men) must remain feminine down to their beautifully-manicured fingertips.

If the saying that 'behind every successful man there is a good woman' is to be believed (and I do not dispute the fact) then surely that woman does not wish to be seen chain-smoking, swigging pints, and swearing like a trooper.

Conversely, if a wife is not content to remain behind her husband, pushing him on in life, whilst she gallantly copes with all the household chores and looking after the family, then as a career girl or business woman she should be duty bound to capitalize on her female charms and remain as feminine as possible.

As a last word (and women usually do have the last word) I think that despite the things we have to endure, to be born a woman is to be truly blessed!

DIANA DORS
*Sunningdale 1983*

# A

*A is for ACROBAT*
The mind boggles when one imagines the kind of tricks HE might perform in bed!

The situation could be equalized of course if SHE were a contortionist!

*A is for ACTORS*
At the risk of upsetting my husband Alan, who is a fine actor, I have to tell you that by and large I think most actors are like overgrown schoolboys playing at being men. I have not always felt like that so it must be a sign of getting older and wiser.

Humphrey Bogart, Errol Flynn and Robert Mitchum belong to the days when actors were men. Whether they were real men or not doesn't matter because they had such magic. These days we are also expected to watch some young actor playing a real he-man role knowing very well he's a self-confessed gay!

Actors work hard and play hard. Hell-raisers like Richard Harris, Peter Finch and Trevor Howard made fascinating reading when their antics reached the papers. It was all down to drink, of course. Why actors drink has to be something to do with the stress of trying to turn in a superb performance and the insecurity of not knowing where the next part is coming from.

But drinking isn't the be-all and end-all of an actor's existence. Most of them are highly nervous, intense, immensely talented people who really only come to life when they step out on stage or in front of the cameras.

Dressed in costume, hiding under make-up and immersed in the character he is playing, an actor can truly let himself go. Once in the dressing room he can become as shy and awkward as any other man.

Falling in love with an actor is a dangerous thing from a girl's point of view, because she never knows whether he means those poetic words of undying love or whether they are just an excerpt from some play he did!

I've got a few good friends who are actors but most of them are, well, just acting!

## A is for ADAM
Adam was the first man – and doesn't he have a lot to answer for? I'll bet there isn't a time in your life when you haven't once wished Adam had never met up with Eve!

Still, if it hadn't been for Adam, I wouldn't be writing this book about men, would I?

## A is for MOHAMMAD ALI
The greatest of his time professionally, and a good-looker too!

However, I wonder how *great* his first wife thought he was when he ditched her and the children for another woman? It is to be hoped that whilst she counted her million dollar ALImony, she felt the great relief of not having to listen to his poems any more.

## A is for ADAM ANT
Adam chose me to be his Fairy Godmother on a video film which was being made in connection with his record 'Prince Charming'. It went to number one and that meant I was on *Top of the Pops* for five weeks. Which just goes to show that getting involved with an

Adam means, if nothing else, you get to appear on Top of the Pops.

We had never met before but Adam wanted me to play his Fairy Godmother, despite my lack of ability as far as magic goes.

Adam Ant is lovely, very professional and very intelligent – for a pop star. That is not to say that all pop stars are stupid, but he is very clever and knows exactly what he's doing and where he's going, so I have great respect for him.

Adam was the first male and Adam Ant was the first male pop star to wear exotic make-up. It's always good to be a forerunner. I was the first sex symbol England ever produced and it was even more exciting because I *was* the first. There have been many since me, of course.

I liked working with Adam Ant and even though our paths have not crossed since the video, he sends me cards from all over the place, wherever he is appearing, and flowers for my birthday. He's high on my pop charts.

## A is for ADONIS

The original pretty boy. In fact, he was fancied by Venus but killed by a bear while out hunting one day. When George IV was Prince Regent a man was sent to prison for calling HRH an 'Adonis of 50'. That hardly seems an imprisonable offence – especially these days when any man, of any age, would take it as a compliment to be called an Adonis.

## A is for ADULTERERS

If you still doubt that it is a man's world, how come it was always the women who got stoned in biblical days for adultery? They had to have men with whom to do it, and I'll bet most of *them* were married!

## A is for AGA KHAN

The late Aga, the present Aga Khan's grandfather, was a sweet old man. I actually had the pleasure of lunching with him at his luxurious villa, with its indoor and outdoor swimming pools, overlooking Cannes.

The South of France resort was packed with stars for the Cannes Film Festival and the Aga invited some of us to lunch with him and his wife, the Begum. Susan Hayward, Ginger Rogers and Richard Todd were in the party.

I'll never forget that day. We not only ate off solid gold plates, but the knives and forks were solid gold as well. I think that occasion was the last he gave for visiting celebrities as he was in poor health and died not long after.

Although I was nervous at meeting such a rich and important man, we were not lost for conversation. It turned out he was fascinated by birds – the feathered kind – and as I had a mischievous cockatoo then, I kept the Aga amused by telling him stories about the bird's habits and tricks.


## A is for PRINCE ALBERT

If only he was alive today the Prince might be able to pass on some advice as to how to keep a woman happy. Queen Victoria was absolutely besotted with him, so much so that she insisted on various monuments being built in his memory like the Royal Albert Hall and the Albert Memorial – and then went into mourning for many years after his death, refusing even to go out.

But he must have been one helluva lover! He fathered nine children (that we know about) and to this day there is still an erection to his memory.

The Christmas Tree which goes up in thousands of homes reminds us that it was dear old Prince Albert who first introduced Christmas Trees to this country.

*A is for ALCOHOLICS*

Alcoholism is more rife today than it has ever been.

A drunken woman is bad enough, but a drunken man is *terrifying*. Many become 'fighting' drunk, battering their wives and children as a result.

It is no good pleading with them to stop drinking, threatening to leave home, or contemplating divorce (even if they are filled with remorse the next day). Until a man accepts the fact that he is an alcoholic and needs help, then a woman has lost her battle against the bottle.

I knew a good Catholic couple once. They had two beautiful little girls and were perfectly happy until the husband started drinking heavily. No amount of begging by the wife, children, or their local priest could stop him, and the marriage deteriorated. When I saw the poor wretch – and I choose my words with care, as alcoholism is a sickness for which there is no cure – helping the priest at the altar and trying to behave in a somewhat sanctimonious manner, when only the night before he had wrenched the youngest child from her mother's arms in a fit of drunken violence, I felt sick in my heart.

Sadly, the story, like some others, did not have a happy ending, for the couple, despite their strong Catholic marriage ties, divorced. The wife was forced into circumstances far removed from her original lifestyle and had to struggle to bring up her family, whilst the husband continued his drinking.

The difference between her plight, and that of other women who might have been able to do better by getting legal help when separating from their alcoholic menfolk, was that he practised as a solicitor, so in his sober, working hours he was able to counteract her every move, and subsequently ruin her life completely.

*A is for ALEXANDER THE CORRECTOR*
Who thinks graffiti is new? This eighteenth-century Bible nut, whose real name was Alexander Cruden, used to go around with a wet sponge wiping graffiti off walls. He'd have a full time job now wouldn't he? I wonder if Kilroy was around then?

*A is for AMERICANS*
I agree with the well-known wit who once said 'America is the only country recorded in history that has gone from barbarism to decadence, without ever having achieved greatness'!

*A is for IDI AMIN*
On the subject of tyrannical madmen, how about this one as a prize example of the type of husband a woman might be unfortunate enough to have?

It is all very well saying 'Yes', but who would marry *him*? Several did, and one was murdered for her trouble! Which just goes to show there is no accounting for taste.

*A is for EAMONN ANDREWS*
I'm dealing with Irishmen under I but I would like to mention Eamonn here. He has brought a great deal of happiness to so many people by flying relatives from foreign shores to meet up again with victims of *This is Your Life*, who otherwise could never have been reunited.

I've been a victim twice now, but I just wish Eamonn could gain more confidence instead of shaking with nerves all through the show. It is a bit disconcerting and quite unnecessary after all these years.

*A is for AQUARIUS*
An Aquarian man will promise you the moon, and really mean to give it to you, IF his everlasting dreaming comes true. Furthermore he will constantly keep asking how you feel towards him, for he *has* to know where he stands in your affections, but NEVER commit himself to you, if he can get away with it.

*A is for ARCHBISHOP*
In 1960 the then Archbishop of Canterbury saw fit to denounce me from the pulpit as a wanton hussy – and all because I had written my life story for the *News of the World*.

What an uproar I caused. Of course, this was before Christine Keeler overthrew the Conservative Government, before the Great Train Robbers, the Beatles and the permissive society.

So my revelations not only shocked the Archbishop, and Randolph Churchill who criticized me on television, but had the whole country taking sides.

When I was chosen for the Royal Variety Performance that year, some pressmen looking for a sensational story rang the Palace press office to see if I might be banned from appearing.

They were told the Royal Family saw no reason to do so and on the contrary were looking forward to the show, whatever I had written about myself.

Obviously the Royals were not the prim and proper fuddy-duddies the newspapers often made them out to be and certainly had a much less narrow outlook than the Archbishop.

*A is for ARIES*
I do not know much about Ariean men but the one thing I would be sure to remember when dealing with them is, never to turn my back! . . . not with that zodiac sign!

*A is for ARTHUR ASKEY*

For a little man he had enormous stamina, and he never gave up. When he was 80 he was still doing a 40-minute solo spot in summer season in Paignton and at 81 he was appearing twice a day in pantomime at Richmond.

Sadly, his legs gave up as he always joked they would and he died in 1982. He had many friends in showbusiness and he is greatly missed.

I am convinced that when Arthur made it to the gates of heaven (he was a religious man and surely would go nowhere else) he waved St Peter aside and yelled 'Hello Playmates!'

*A is for AUSTRALIANS*

Only a woman with masochistic tendencies could fall in love with some of these rough, beer-swilling men, whose manners are fit only for the outback, and whose coarse humour belongs to the lowest type of 'stag night' gathering imaginable.

Women outnumber men four to one in Australia according to statistics, so unfortunately they have to put up with all sorts of indignities if they want a mate . . . personally, I would rather remain a spinster!

*A is for AYATOLLAH (KHOMEINI)*

This has got to be the most sinister looking man ever! It is hard to imagine him as a baby (certainly one only a mother could love I'm sure) and even harder to imagine him as a young man fooling around with females. Perhaps he never did . . . Indeed I cannot imagine him doing anything that is in any way human, and if I had to name a man who gave me nightmares, the Ayatollah with his grim black hat, long beard, and beady eyes, would take precedence over every other tyrant in history.

# B

## B is for BALD MEN

They say baldness is a sign of virility. As I've never been to bed with a bald man I cannot confirm that. However, there *is* something very sexy about a man's bald head.

I never understand why men like Bobby Charlton and Arthur Scargill go to such great lengths to persuade a couple of strands of hair to stay in place over their ever-widening bald patch.

If only they went bald gracefully, they might even become a couple of sex symbols like Kojak!

## B is for BARBERS

Disregarding 'Teasy-Weasy' Raymond whom I used to call 'the Demon Barber', and, of course, the most famous of them all, Sweeney Todd, I'll bet most barbers could tell a few stories. Get a man in the chair and he reveals all! I once knew a young reporter who had the best turned out head of hair in Hollywood. He went to his barber at least twice a week, got the man talking and learned all the hot gossip that his other customers had spilled.

As Warren Beatty depicted in the film 'Shampoo', male ladies' hairdressers, obviously have something that is attractive to women clients. Look at the number of stars who have had love affairs with theirs – Barbara Streisand for one, and our own Lulu, who actually married her crimper.

## B is for BASTARDS

This is the husband who can just walk away without batting an eyelid. OK, if he's a nice guy he'll send his wife and kids some money, but most of them don't.

Many women devote their whole lives to such men only to be left for a younger version. All I can say is they are better off without these bastards!

## B is for WARREN BEATTY

Warren's good looks and sex appeal have excited female fans since Joan Collins first found him way back in the early sixties, but Joan, like many women since, failed to get him to the altar, and at the time of writing he is still Beatty the Bachelor.

His prowess with the opposite sex is renowned and something of which he is immensely proud. Famous names such as the late Natalie Wood and Lesley Caron were but two to fall for his fatal charm.

Not so this writer however, who found herself pursued by him on two occasions, once in a car on Rodeo Drive, when he pleaded with me to follow him to his house in a nearby canyon, and on another occasion when I was alone in my hotel suite in New York and he threatened, on the telephone, to kick my door in!

Sorry Warren, but this Dors did not swing open on demand.

## B is for BEER-MEN

How they can put away pint after pint of the stuff I'll never understand. At best, to me, it tastes like cold stewed tea and at worst it tastes like dishwater. But men seem to like it – and sadly, most of them grow fat on it.

There are thousands of what I call beer men – the ones who prefer a pint to a woman. They can usually be seen in pubs looking longingly at a frothy head on a pint of beer and raving about how great it looks.

You will never see them fondle their wives in the same way, and they'll never tell a woman she looks beautiful.

Why men are like this is beyond me. Have you ever seen a woman lift up a glass of gin and tonic and say how handsome it looks!

Watching a man take a sip of frothy beer sometimes makes me feel like a voyeur! The look on his face is so ecstatic he might as well be having an orgasm!

Whenever I think of beer-men I immediately conjure up a picture of actor Oliver Reed who I am sure would rather be in a pub swilling beer, or anything else for that matter, than spend his time in the company of women.

I have heard that when Olly has had a few he insists on trying to drink a yard of ale and after that has been known to try to climb up the nearest chimney. Obviously, he thinks he's Father Christmas!

Obviously to his type a woman is just a convenience. She must be there just to make sure he gets home all right. And I wonder if it is worth it? What kind of lover is any man who has just sunk eight pints and tried to climb up the chimney going to be?

*B is for JACK BENNY*
The marvellous American comedian who based a great deal of his act on pretending to be the meanest man in the world. In real life he was far from mean, and before his death gave so much to millions, not only in money but in pleasure and happiness.

I was once asked to appear on his television show in Hollywood, and a sample of the exquisite Benny humour, dry, and outwardly serious, happened on the first morning we assembled to rehearse. As we began to read through the script, Jack suddenly paused and, looking up with a very straight expression, said, 'Excuse me, but does anyone here know how tall a penguin is?' We were all mystified; not only was nobody an authority on penguins, but the question had come completely out of the blue. Several people proffered suggestions, although they obviously had not the slightest idea what they were talking about, and gradually a serious discussion grew about the size and width of the birds. All the while Jack parried and answered questions, putting forth his own ideas as to how high the things stood. Finally it was decided by a maximum vote that they could not possibly be taller than a foot and a half, if that. Jack sat back with a large grin all over his face and sighed, 'Oh dear, then it must have been a nun I ran over in my car this morning.'

After the show had been completed I received a set of photographs of he and I, which I kept along with all the thousands of others I had acquired in my life. One day, years later, I had the idea of putting about a hundred up on the walls of the billiard room in my home. They were very interesting for people who played the game to look at whilst waiting for their turn, as literally everyone I had worked with was there – stars and scenes from films and shows over my thirty years in show-business. Naturally they were valuable as, like everything else, the older they got, the more interesting they became. Of course, they could never be replaced.

Once I decided in a mad moment to give Alan a Great Dane puppy for his birthday, and after great research and trouble I bought a magnificent champion with a pedigree to match, and named him Tiberius. Alan was delighted, but as Tiberius was not house trained, we bedded him down at night in the billiard room, carefully covering the carpet with newspaper – as like the dog, it was very expensive!

Time went on and Tiberius had still not learned his

social graces. He was always ripping up the news-papers and, much to our dismay, the carpet under-neath. The final straw came one morning when I heard Alan shout from below my bedroom.

'Whatever's the matter?' I called out as he reached the bottom of the stairs.

'Darling, the most terrible thing has happened,' he exclaimed dramatically.

'What is it?' I asked, almost too scared to want to know, and visualizing the poor dog ill, or perhaps even dead . . . 'Tiberius has just eaten Jack Benny,' he cried.

### B is for GEORGE BEST
He has my great sympathy because of his struggle with alcoholism. There is not a great deal more to be said, except that I pray that he will be able to conquer such a terrible illness. George is too talented and too handsome to allow the Devil's fluid to destroy him altogether.

### B is for BLUE JOKERS
Whenever anyone mentions blue jokers I always remember the greatest of them all, Max Miller. He was an incredible character. I first met him when I was appearing in variety at the Hippodrome in Brighton, which was his home town, and he came to see me.

Max was very mean and also quite proud of the fact that he had never bought anyone a drink or, indeed, anything at all!

When John Osborne created the character Archie Rice in 'The Entertainer' he had Max Miller in mind, and Sir Laurence Olivier, having been asked to play the failed comedian, studied Miller on stage.

He is known even now as the Cheeky Chappie because his act *was* cheeky. Stories about Max Miller abound, many of them untrue, but I think the best one I ever heard came from the man's own lips.

Towards the end of his career Max had been asked to appear in the Royal Variety Performance and Val Parnell who was running the show, as always, lectured him sternly: 'The Royal Family are going to be there and you must not be dirty. No way can you use any jokes from your little blue book, you've got to keep the act clean.

'Promise me, swear to me that you will.'

Max agreed fairly solemnly.

But on the night Val Parnell was still in such a nervous state that he ran around to Max's dressing room and repeated his order. 'Remember all I've said. No blue jokes!'

Whereupon Max promptly went out on stage and told every one he had in his little blue book.

Val Parnell was furious. He rushed backstage and, thumping on the dressing room door, shouted, 'You bastard, you told me you weren't going to do any blue jokes. You promised me you were going to keep it clean and what do you do? You bring out every dirty one you can find!

'Well that's it, you have cooked your goose. You are *finished* in show business. I'll make sure you never work in any of my theatres again. What do you think of that?'

'You're about £375,000 too late,' replied the cheeky old joker gleefully.

*B is for HUMPHREY BOGART*

It is not widely known, except by those who worked closely with him, that this brilliant actor, and suave star of films like *Casablanca*, had a habit of picking his nose.

Perhaps that is why they nicknamed him Bogie?

## B is for ERNEST BORGNINE

Although he looks so menacing, Ernie is one of the most gentle actors it has been my privilege to work with. We made a film with Raquel Welch in Spain and while Raquel was busy looking at herself in the mirror (her favourite occupation – and I am not being bitchy), Ernie, the rest of the cast and I, played cards and dined out in good restaurants, regaling each other with stories and experiences. Ernie was then married to a girl who had been, he told me, a stand-in for me when I first went to Hollywood.

In fact Ernie had been married several times, once to the Mexican actress Katy Jurado, and once to Ethel Merman. His first wife was not an actress. He has since been married again, and I find it a continual source of mystery as to what goes wrong with Ernie's marriages. At the time he always seems so devoted.

When Ernie's filming had finished in Spain he came round to say his goodbyes, and it was then he told me of one of his pet grievances. 'It really bugs me,' he said. 'They get you to agree to do a movie and you sign the contract; they then fly you out to some foreign location where the director, producer and production manager all meet you on the tarmac as your plane lands, shake you by the hand and tell you what a thrill and honour it is to have you on the film, then they drive you in style in a big limousine to the hotel, and so you work your guts out away from your home and children until the big day comes and it's all over. Then suddenly something happens – they have had your life's blood, they've had your contracted work and best, but the producer and the director always seem to be missing on your last day! And the production guy says, 'Hey sorry we got no car to take you to the airport, but they're all out on location, would you mind taking a taxi?' So there you are jogging along some road to the airport in a cab, wondering what you did or did not do

23

that warranted no star treatment on the way back like you had when you first arrived.'

I knew only too well what he meant as it had happened to me and others too many times. It makes you feel like yesterday's laundry! To this day, if Alan, myself or any actor friends get the taxi routine worked on us whilst on location, we call it 'doing an Ernest Borgnine'. Recently I watched a re-run of one of his films, *The Vikings*, on TV and after seeing his last horrifying death scene, in which he leaps into a pit of wolves who tear him to pieces, I could not help turning to Alan and saying, 'I suppose when that was done, Ernie was to be seen jogging along a Norwegian road to Oslo in a taxi.' Thank goodness only actors know about the seamier side of show business otherwise it would certainly spoil the illusion for the general public.

## B is for BOSSY MEN

'No wife of mine will ever work,' the bossy man says. 'No wife of mine will wear that,' he goes on. Bossy men are so irritating. I'm no women's libber but I rebelled against this type long ago.

My father would never let my mother work and when she had her waist-length hair cut into a twenties bob he refused to talk to her for three weeks. I decided there was no way I would ever take orders from any man.

I think that relationships are all about communicating and compromise and no one partner should be allowed to lay down the law to the other.

## B is for SCOTT BRADY

Scott is an actor who sadly, through no fault of his own, never made it as a really big star. He was as handsome as it is possible to be when he arrived in Hollywood, the younger brother of the late Lawrence Tierney who had made such a great hit in movies with his first film *Dillinger* – the story of the notorious American gangster. Scott was a good professional actor who knew the ropes, so to speak, was always handy with stunt work, which saved the studios extra money, and was never late 'on set' (an unforgiveable crime in films) in spite of his love of drinking and womanizing. But with the luck of the show business draw he never got to the top and remained slogging away in what were known as 'B' pictures. His one great chance came, he thought, when he was cast for the lead opposite Jane Russell in a film entitled *Gentlemen Marry Brunettes*, a follow-up to Marilyn Monroe's successful *Gentlemen Prefer Blondes*. I worked with Scott many years later on a Hitchcock television series and found him a great character to act with, and to have fun with during our leisure hours. He had a wonderful sense of humour and, in spite of his reputation as a bit of a hell-raiser and drinker, I found he had an extremely intelligent mind, and knew a great deal about Shakespeare and classical literature. He would regale me with stories which were always entertaining. One of them concerned the film I have just mentioned, or at least something that happened whilst he was in England doing it.

He arrived in England where the film was to be made and was given the star treatment, including a luxurious suite in a top London hotel. All went well; Scott revelled in the whole venture; and for the first time in his career he played it like a star. One evening he and his stand-in were driving up Park Lane with nothing in particular to do, when he had the idea of picking up a couple of prostitutes and taking them back to the exclusive hotel, not for sex, but in order to give them a really good evening's 'pleasure and rest' as he put it. As they entered the lobby the hall porter, who was kitted out in silken knee breeches and wore a permanently disdainful expression on his face, looked horrified at the sight of what he obviously recognized straight away as two ladies of the night being brought into the palatial establishment.

Scott ordered him to send champagne and a banquet-style supper up to his suite, and they proceeded to the lift despite the porter's obvious disgust at the situation. The night went well; Scott was in sparkling form; and after plying the girls with food and drink, he quoted poetry, acted scenes from some of his films, told jokes and generally gave them an evening which they had never had before, and certainly did not expect.

Finally, at around three a.m. he collapsed, weary and tired with the whole project and politely informed them that they had better think about leaving, as he had an early call at the studio and would have to go to bed.

The girls looked astounded, and one of them rather cheekily asked, 'Well, what about our money?'

'What do you mean money?' asked Scott incredulously. 'You've had a great evening haven't you? Champagne, the works and we've tried to keep you amused and give you a good time.'

'I'm glad you said that,' she replied, 'You've had our time you mean, and we want paying for it. It don't matter what you have or have not done to us, but you've had us up here taking up our time and stopping us from earning, so we want our money.'

Scott could see trouble brewing, so he went into the bedroom and called down to the desk, the silk knee-breeched porter picked up the phone. 'Had enough, sir?' he enquired sarcastically.

'Yes,' said Scott. 'Come up here and get these dames out, they're causing trouble and refusing to leave.'

What followed next can only be described as pandemonium. The porter arrived hot-foot, eager to carry out Scott's wishes, and also delighted to prove that he had been right in his appraisal of the girls in the first place. They started screaming and lashing out at Scott, his stand-in and the porter, both verbally and physically, demanding their money and using extremely abusive language in the process. Somehow, in spite of his elegant costume, and aristocratic air, the porter managed to manhandle them, one under each arm, to the doorway of the suite. As each colourful adjective was hurled at Scott and his friend he managed to keep shushing them by telling them it was an exclusive hotel and he did not want the other residents awakened by their barrage of abuse.

As the porter dragged them down the corridor the one who had raised the issue about payment and time in the first place broke free from his grasp and, realizing that she was not going to get her money, decided to deliver one last blast at her former host.

'Call yourself a star,' she shouted, arms akimbo. 'I've had dukes and earls . . . and Donald Peers!'

*B is for BRICKLAYERS*
Just be careful he doesn't huff and puff and blow your house down!

*L is for LENNY BRUCE*
They made a film about him; he wrote his book which shocked many people. But that is how he spent his life, shocking people – usually hypocrites who did not like what they heard him say, for it was always the truth. I am speaking of course of the one and only Lenny Bruce, my dear friend who killed himself due to a tragic hang-up with drugs – a state brought about through no fault of his own. Like many ex-servicemen fighting for their country, having been badly wounded he became hooked on the morphine he was given to ease the pain.

My first meeting with Lenny was in New York where he was appearing in a small dark nightclub, and I thought his was the most brilliant comedy act I had ever heard. Lenny's scene, his comedy and thinking, was totally different from anyone, and most of it was drawn from his experiences of life. I was in New York doing one of their top television shows – the Steve Allen Show – and Lenny had been booked by Steve, a shrewd judge of talent. Everyone thought Steve Allen had lost his mind by doing this as Lenny was unreliable, completely impossible to rehearse, and used material which was wickedly humorous but involved the use of many four-letter words.

Lenny was far from being an idiot, though, and he appreciated and respected Steve's trust in him so the show, thankfully, went without a flaw.

He attempted to enter England around the time of the Christine Keeler affair but the powers that be would not let him in. His escapades in cities like Chicago, where he was threatened with being found in an alley should he dare to come there again, were as famous as his act. The number of places he was allowed to perform in grew less and less, and the wine of success began to turn sour.

However, one incident did occur in a Las Vegas hotel when I was present. I was not with his party but sitting in front of him watching a very funny comedian, Shecky Greene, doing his act. Lenny got very exuberant and, although his wife tried to shut him up, let forth a loud stream of four-letter heckling to Shecky, who defended himself well. The whole evening was extremely funny. The management were not so amused, however, and by tricking him to the telephone saying there was a call, they ordered him out of the establishment for ever! No doubt angry about this affair, and high on drugs, Lenny then went on to another hotel, the Flamingo, where Pearl Bailey was performing. Unable to stand her 'Uncle Tom' style of entertainment he leapt on to the stage, grabbed a fire extinguisher and, pointing it at Pearl, let her have it right in the face! 'Oh my Lord, my Lord,' cried Pearl, and as pandemonium broke out he was led away. I believe he actually sat down and wrote her a letter saying how disgusted he was with her act. He could not abide her 'shtick', as he put it, which involved pushing parts of her body into customers' faces. He had his opinion of what was right and wrong on stage and in life, but nevertheless he was escorted to the Las Vegas border by a gun-toting sheriff and told never to enter the state of Nevada again.

I loved him, and my fondest memories were not of the Lenny who shocked and stormed audiences on stage, but the quiet, almost elfin-like person who would turn up at my Beverly Hills home in jeans and whizz me off on the back of his motorcycle to proudly show me his brand new home with the swimming pool, no furniture, and a large orange pumpkin standing by the fireplace. Lenny, you are sadly missed, and today no one would be startled by your antics – but like many great talents you were born before your time.

## B is for RICHARD BURTON

Despite his acting talent and rich Welsh speaking voice, one wonders just how far Richard Burton's film career would have gone if he had not married Elizabeth Taylor, as before he met her his track record was down to starring in poorly made screen offerings like *Ice Palace*, a modest low-budget affair.

Burton had the gall, after ditching his long-suffering wife Sybil in favour of Liz – and I say long-suffering because she coped with him whilst he went through some of Hollywood's beautiful women during their marriage – to telephone her one day, as he had heard a rumour that she was enjoying herself around New

York with the handsome young man who became her second husband.

Although Sybil had endured public humiliation and private misery over his affair with La Taylor, she still dutifully endured his questions regarding her welfare, and when asked about the young man in question, replied it was 'merely a bit of harmless fun' which, heaven knows, she was entitled to.

'Sybil,' said Burton solemnly, with the air of a Victorian husband, 'I sincerely hope you are BEHAVING yourself!'

### B is for BUS CONDUCTORS

In the old days there used to be a bus conductors' joke – 'How far will you let me go for fourpence?'

Of course one would not get far for fourpence in this day and age, but if a bus conductor does offer you a free ride, you can be sure there will be some sort of price to pay at the end.

Come to think of it, men are somewhat like buses themselves . . . if you miss one, there is always another coming along behind!

### B is for BUTCHERS

I cannot imagine what going to bed with a butcher is like, but I do know that if I did I would never get over the fear that he might handle me rather the same way he does those carcasses in the shop – or worse still, compare me with one!

### B is for BUTLERS

I would not like to have lived under the sort of regime Gordon Jackson imposed as Mr Hudson in the television series Upstairs, Downstairs, even though he portrayed the type of servant who faded away all too quickly after the Great War. Loyal and utterly trustworthy.

Butlers to this day, however, are still rather haughty, aloof characters, who make their employers feel inferior, let alone any other servants.

But they are also human when all is said and done, and aside from being made the butt of jokes of the 'What the butler saw' variety, they belong to that close-knit, tight-lipped and 'never let a woman know the real truth' fraternity, known as MEN!

A certain story is told regarding one well-known Duke, which might shock Hudson, but says much for the secrecy which is prevalent between master and servant, regardless of that tight inner circle of men.

It seems his Lordship awoke one morning feeling rather fruity and, summoning his trusty to the bed-chamber, asked what he could do about the somewhat large bump under the sheets. Without batting an eyelid, the butler replied, 'Shall I inform her Ladyship sir, or would you prefer me to smuggle it into London?'

# C

## C is for CAESAR

He came, he saw, he conquered – and not just the British. The saying goes: 'Julius Caesar was every man's wife and every wife's husband.' It was no surprise then, that he wound up getting stabbed in the back?

## C is for JAMES CAGNEY

When he pushed that grapefruit in *May Bush*'s face Jimmy was epitomizing one of the mysteries of all time – why do ladies prefer bastards?

Most women at some time in their lives have fallen hook, line and sinker for an absolute rotter, and I'm no exception. Everyone else can see he is no good but love is definitely blind.

Love is also misguided. It makes you think that if you love a man enough he'll stop being a bastard and become all sweetness and light. However, if they were all like James Cagney in real life, none of us would have cause for concern. I think he's sensational!

## C is for CALIGULA

The most insane Roman Emperor of all, 'Little Boots' as he was nicknamed even made his horse a Senator! As if that was not enough, he gave it a manger of ivory and a golden goblet to drink from. But, compared with some of his incestuous, murderous acts, this was child's play – the type of child only a mother could love, and I have my doubts about Caligula's!

## C is for CANCER

Cancerians are extremely sensitive men and must be handled very carefully. The martyrdom from which they suffer manifests itself in childhood and goes on growing steadily worse as they get older. However, the most important thing for any woman to remember, if married or involved emotionally with one of them, is that although they love their homes and regard them as a shell with which to shield themselves from the outside world, they are also capable of using some other woman's home in exactly the same way before returning to their own . . . IF they do.

## C is for CAPRICORN

Capricorn men are the most sexually attractive of all the signs. At least, that is my own personal opinion. Maybe I find them so attractive because I admire their total determination to attain what they want, and, unlike Scorpio men, they are not ruthless or possessive. However the determination they possess does make them rather arrogant and infuriating, for regardless of how good a fight women may put up, these men always get their way in the end! One further warning – females should always remember that a Capricorn never lets his left hand know what his right one is doing!

## C is for CHARLIE CHAPLIN

He was not only extremely funny, but one of the first and greatest exponents of slapstick comedy which has lasted even until today. People still imitate Chaplin: he will never be forgotten.

## C is for CHARLES II

The last words this merry monarch uttered on his death bed were 'Let not poor Nelly starve', meaning his mistress, Nell Gwynn, the orange seller. I wonder how many other men have given their mistresses a final thought at the end?

## C is for MALE CHAUVINISTS
Many women have already written at length about such men, and indeed I am not doing badly myself thus far, so I will not elaborate further on the subject, except to say . . . carry on reading, and you'll find they still keep popping up!

## C is for MAURICE CHEVALIER
Unlike most of the women in the world who were absolutely besotted with this smooth French charmer, I never liked Maurice Chevalier. But then, Frenchmen hold no fascination for me and I'll be dealing with then later in the book.

Chevalier was accused of being a Nazi collaborator which tarnished his reputation and after the war his career lapsed somewhat until *Gigi* in 1958 put him back at the top. After that he enjoyed great success right up to the time of his death.

He will go down in history as one of the all-time greats, but, frankly, what women saw in him I'll never know.

## C is for WINSTON CHURCHILL
There were many who hated him, calling him a warmonger amongst other things, but here was a man who led us through hell with fine speeches to strengthen our morale. It was his dogged tenacity which enabled us to enjoy our finest hour of victory.

Churchill was a strange mixture of bulldog ruthlessness, hard-drinking cynicism, and great artistry. Painting was his favourite hobby.

Where women were concerned, he did not seem to score, indeed he showed no interest in them other than his beloved Clemmie, but of all the witticisms accredited to him, one of the best involved a lady of no lesser physical proportions than himself, the late Bessie Braddock MP.

Bessie was a fat, somewhat coarse looking woman, who had gained a seat in the House of Commons. During her time she had many a shouting match with Churchill – in fact their rows became quite an everyday occurrence there.

On one of these occasions, a really bad argument ensued between them, so heated that Churchill lost his temper and publicly insulted her.

'Madam. You are UGLY,' he said.

'And you, Mr Churchill, are DRUNK,' retorted the outraged Bessie.

'Yes, but in the morning I will be sober,' he snapped back.

## C is for NAT 'KING' COLE

When Nat 'King' Cole died I think the world of music lost one of the greatest singers it has ever known, and to this day I still cannot believe he has left us; his voice is immortal. Way back early in 1952, for the first time since the war, British bands were beginning to invade America, and our best was undoubtedly Ted Heath's band. They had been booked for a big performance in Georgia and starring with them was Nat 'King' Cole. The hall was packed to capacity. Ted Heath and his band played for the entire first half, storming the audience and no doubt feeling very pleased with themselves – quite rightly! After the interval the 'King' began his act and all went well until suddenly two men (possibly Ku Klux Klan members) rushed on to the stage and knocked him down. Pandemonium followed, fighting breaking out everywhere. The Ted Heath band sat frozen on stage not knowing what to do. Suddenly Ted had a brainwave, or so he thought, and shouted, 'Play God Save the Queen!' They obeyed instantly, but with all due respect, our National Anthem was hardly going to quell a race riot in Georgia! No-one was listening. As the strains of 'God Save Our Gracious Queen' pervaded the hall, Nat's terrified manager who was hiding in the wings, screamed out to the British band, 'Fuck the Queen, the King is on the floor!!!!.'

## C is for COMEDIANS

Heaven help any woman who is married to a comedian, and I should know – I had one for a second husband.

These 'funny men' may be highly amusing in company, and indeed many of them are friends of mine, but at home most of them can be miserable devils!

The late Will Hay was reputed to be moody and sullen to live with.

W. C. Fields hated EVERYBODY, on top of his famed dislike of children and animals.

Groucho Marx even humiliated his bride at the altar during their wedding ceremony, for when asked if he would 'take her for better or worse' he finally replied, after a long pause, 'I'm thinking it over.' Later, at the reception, the unfortunate woman fell through the seat of a wicker chair, and lay sprawled in a most unflattering position. Without attempting to help her up, Groucho shouted, 'I've told you a dozen times, that isn't funny!'

When the late British comedian Dave Morris introduced himself to people he always added, 'This is the wife . . . don't laugh!' But by the same token Frank 'It's the way I tell 'em' Carson's wife actually maintains that he cracks jokes from morning till night, and carries on in that ebullient manner all the time.

If this is true, then in an odd way she is one of the lucky ones (though I cannot imagine how exhausting living with such a man must be) for most comedians are very serious, rather insecure people at heart, and I am not referring to the 'sad mask of the clown' which they often display to the world when things are bad.

One famed British comedian who has a reputation for

being extremely mean financially, declined to marry the woman in his life (claiming that he'd have to pay more tax if he did!) but insisted that the poor woman devote herself so totally to him that she even had to stand in the wings during his act with a stop-watch, timing the length of laughs his jokes received at every performance.

Another comic, now sadly passed on, was not only a misery to live with, having his meals, watching television and sleeping alone, but guarded his money so carefully that instead of employing a hairdresser and a boy scout, to wash his car and give his hair a trim in that order, insisted on his wife doing it, and gave her the equivalent of fifty pence in old currency for each job.

The list of comedians who have since passed on to the great stage in the sky, and whose careers and marriages were beset with misery, neurosis, and paranoia during their lifetime, is endless.

Tony Hancock, Peter Sellers, Arthur 'Old Mother Riley' Lucan, Bud Abbott, Charlie Chaplin, Stan Laurel, Oliver Hardy, Fatty Arbuckle, and our own George Formby are merely an isolated few who knew the heartache of what it takes to make people laugh whilst their words were falling apart, either from the merciless, tough competition of the comedy business (fiercest of all artistic professions) or the emotional domestic tangles which left some of them also financially destitute, due to hefty alimony payments.

Endless too are the comedians both here and in America, who have long since failed to make their wives laugh, and thus taken mistresses ready to chuckle at anything they say. In fairness to those supposedly 'non-understanding' wives, I have to say, 'How often can *anyone* be expected to react favourably to the same gags?'

It was with a twinge of cynicism that I once read a press quote from Anthea Redfern, when she became Bruce Forsyth's second wife.

'Bruce is so wonderful, he keeps me in fits of laughter

all the time,' she enthused. 'Most evenings we are happiest just having a candlelit dinner alone together, sitting by the fire with a bottle of wine, and talking way into the night. He is SUCH an amusing man.'

My cynicism was sadly proved right, for less than a year after I read about such apparent marital bliss with a comedian, they were divorced!

## C is for SEAN CONNERY

Sean Connery is an old and very 'natural' friend of mine. He comes from Scotland and is completely honest – and sometimes blunt or hurtful – in the things he says, but at least you know where you stand with him. He is not a hypocrite. But like everyone else in the world of show business he is human and will only take just so much before he finally snaps. One such incident occurred when we all went to a big boxing match between Mohammed Ali and Henry Cooper. We had paid hefty prices for the seats – around fifty pounds each as I recall – and everyone in our party was a celebrity. There was a lot of fuss and autograph signing when we sat down before the fight commenced. But eventually we settled back to enjoy ourselves. The lights went up, and the magnificent Ali made his entrance. The air of excitement was electric. Barely halfway through the first round a woman suddenly came rushing up to Sean and I and shoved a book under our noses to sign, completely obscuring our view! Had she offered it to me first I suppose I would have laboriously agreed, but unfortunately for her she aimed it at Sean.

With typical Scots candour, and without too much restraint in his voice, he snapped, 'Get out of my bloody way woman. Do you think I've paid fifty quid a seat to sit here and look at you?'

I wondered if she ever went to see a James Bond film again!

## C is for COOKS
No, I haven't got it wrong. All the world's top chefs are men . . . so the question I want to ask is, how come most of them claim they can't cook?

## C is for COUNTS
These days there are very few around, which is probably why the title is now associated with impoverished European aristocracy, and has no great significance at all.

Which brings me to a silly little story that really sums up the title.

Two out of work actors met in the street one day, and began discussing their careers.

One said glumly that he was doing nothing in particular at the time, whilst the other stated that, due to a lack of work, he had joined a theatre group who were producing a play entitled 'I Killed the Count', currently showing in the West End.

'But that's great,' said the first actor. 'What exactly are you doing in it?'

'I'm an O watcher for the neon light company,' the other replied sadly.

## C is for SIR NOEL COWARD
I was lucky to have met this brilliant man briefly, and I'm sure these two favourite stories about him are true. The now sadly late David Niven was complaining to Noel one day that all his friends seemed to be dying or dead.

'My dear boy,' said Coward in his famous drawl, 'I count myself very lucky if mine last until lunchtime!'

On another occasion Noel was on the balcony of a friend's house in Brighton, watching the passers-by with a small boy who was also a house guest.

As they looked down on the pavement they saw two dogs making love. The little boy asked Noel what the dogs were doing.

With just a momentary pause Noel answered, 'Well, you see my boy, the dog in front is blind and the one at the back is very kindly pushing him all the way to St Dunstan's.'

## C is for COWBOYS

The type of cowboys as portrayed on screen in the old days, like William 'Hopalong Cassidy' Boyd and Roy Rogers, I have to say, never turned me on. The only ones I ever met in real life were the 'Midnight Cowboy' types who, frankly, left a great deal to be desired.

There was only one who made my heart beat faster, as I watched him striding through a whole series of spaghetti Westerns, namely sexy Clint Eastwood.

Here was a strong, silent man, who on film would never desert a lady in her hour of need and whose private life, appeared to be (rather like Robert Redford's) impeccable where women, other than his wife, were concerned.

Alas, Clint turned out to be like all the rest! Having been married for many years, he left her for someone else, thus proving sadly that cowboy heroes are really just like ordinary men when they get down off their horses.

## C is for CRICKETERS

This is the game that, even though they are dressed in white, really shows men up in their true colours. Watching a game of cricket is about as exciting as watching paint dry! However many men do find it fascinating.

It seems that once man puts on cricket whites he thinks that he has turned into superman. There was one amateur cricket player who caught the ball in his mouth (not on purpose of course) and was rushed to hospital. (The game went on) After he had had an operation to repair the damage he returned to the pitch to bat. *That's* a fanatic cricketer!

## C is for CRITICS
As the Irish playwright Brendan Behan is reputed to have said: 'Critics are rather like eunuchs: they've seen it done, they know how it should be done, but they cannot do it themselves.'

However, the great composer Sibelius summed them all up accurately enough when he said: 'No-one has ever erected a statue to a critic.'

## C is for OLIVER CROMWELL
As Shakespeare's Mark Antony said, 'the evil that men do lives after them' and this certainly applies to England's only dictator (as portrayed on film by Richard Harris) if the haunting of my house is anything to go by.

Cromwell was a Puritanical man whose principles and ideals may very well have been in the right place, but his beliefs did not give him the go-ahead to destroy and burn, as he did, all the beautiful Catholic churches in the land.

Something dreadful must have occurred on his orders in the church next door to where I now live, for I can only conclude that the place was originally a monastery, and when Cromwell's men came to call not a stick nor stone was left intact. Neither were the poor monks.

Throughout the years I have resided here all kinds of strange happenings have been seen and heard, including the actual sighting once of a monk in robe and sandals. All of which leads me to believe that some unhappy spirits still manifest themselves in my house and grounds from time to time, bewailing the terrible fate Cromwell bestowed upon them.

# D

### D is for LES DAWSON
Once upon a time I was *Mrs* Dawson! However, it was another comedian called Dickie, not Les, whose name I shared. Our marital union could never have happened anyway, as Les has been happily married to *his* Mrs Dawson for many years, so I will just have to be content to share him with her, and the rest of his adoring public, forever.

I think Les Dawson is the best that Britain's got!

### D is for STEVE DAVIS
This is the poor boy who claims he prefers snooker to sex. Has he really ever tried going to bed with a cue?

### D is for DEVIL
I am a little superstitious but the Devil does not frighten me as much as he might have done before I converted to the Catholic faith. However, there is a saying that all women should remember when dealing with men. 'Indifference beats the Devil.' Think about it. It works like a charm.

### D is for DISC JOCKEYS
This is a profession which many people think requires very little talent; indeed, even the best Britain's got, Terry Wogan, once said it did not need much in the way of intelligence to stand in front of a microphone, talk rubbish, and put records on.

However, having been one myself for a brief period,

Terry is actually being unduly modest, for it is not as easy as it looks.

The only thing I have against DJs, as they now slickly call themselves, is the fact that they all seem to be so full of their newly found fame and importance that they talk non-stop gibberish, sometimes doing it through the records which is highly irritating, especially as most of them have nothing of great interest to say.

I wonder if the ex-Mrs Tony Blackburn, Mrs Noel Edmonds, Mrs Jimmy Young and Mrs David 'Diddy' Hamilton would agree with me?'

## D is for DIVORCEES

With the divorce rate in this country at one in three and rising there will soon be more divorcees around than married people.

Men seem to marry for odd reasons.

I have found that some men merely want a woman to wash and iron for them. Others, up and coming businessmen, merely want a pretty hostess to lay on elaborate dinner parties.

A good friend of mine, actress and authoress Pamela Mason, once said that marriage is the first step to divorce. She meant it as a funny remark at the time, but little did she know it would one day backfire on her.

Having driven her husband, actor James Mason, to the airport one day when he was leaving to do a film, she got home to find a writ server on the doorstep with a petition for a divorce. James had filed it before he left, and never breathed a word.

For me the all time divorcee must be Tommy Manville. I've lost count of the number of times he was married and divorced and I don't think he was ever sure either!

43

*D is for DOCTORS*

Happily, I have had nothing but marvellous experiences with doctors who have been involved in my serious illnesses. In fact if it hadn't been for my local GP I wouldn't be alive to write this book.

However, it is an alarming statistic that doctors as a group are high on the list of drug addicts. Let us hope the one in your life is not a Dr Jekyll!

*D is for DOG LOVERS*

It isn't only women who fall for their pooches; there are many men who say 'Love me, love my dog'.

I once knew an actor called Tony Wright who laboured under the title of 'Britain's Mr Beefcake' back in the fifties.

Apart from being married at the time to the late actress Janet Munro he had a female Alsation dog with whom he was absolutely besotted.

Whether the dog was the cause of the breakup of their marriage I have no idea but Tony was totally captivated by it.

She went everywhere with him, slept on his bed, and he talked to her as if she was human. When Tony and Janet split up the dog seemed to be the only thing left for him to love.

On one occasion he was staying at my farmhouse and as I had been invited to dinner by a very wealthy lady I asked Tony if he would like to come along.

By this time the dog was driving everyone mad and I hoped he might leave her at home thus giving us all a break; but no, he brought the animal along.

We dined at a lovely country restaurant where naturally the dog was not allowed, so he asked our hostess if he could leave it outside in her brand new Rolls Royce.

The car was chocolate brown with chocolate brown upholstery to match. It was the lady's pride and joy, but being a dog lover herself – she had FIVE giant poodles – she allowed him to do as he had asked.

After dinner we went outside and found that the worst had happened: the dog had been so upset at being deserted as she thought by her master that she had chewed all the upholstery to shreds.

Tony slumped down by the car, was miserable and inconsolable. But our hostess was marvellous. Not only did she assure him it did not matter and hug the dog, but two days later took him a present of prime steaks for the animal.

I wonder if a male dog love would have done the same?

## D is for KIRK DOUGLAS

My first meeting with this handsome Hollywood superstar was at the home of actor James Mason and his then wife Pamela, later the greatest woman friend I have ever had. But this was 1956, and my first trip to the celluloid city. In those days, Sundays at the Masons were a big social event. Any number of famous folk would be there, arriving at all times of the day and sampling the wonderful hospitality provided. One of the main functions was the tennis. James would organize the proceedings almost as if he were still portraying Rommel, the German Field Marshal he had played in a film some years before. Unless you put your foot down firmly, as Pam did for instance, you were designated to play tennis at any hour and be partnerd off with some of the best players in Hollywood. It was my bad luck that on my first Sunday there I was literally thrown on to the court with who else but Kirk. To make matters worse we were playing against James himself, who fancied his chances very strongly at the game, and Ginger Rogers, a player of professional standard. Now, I had played tennis before, but I was pretty hopeless at it. I always looked good in the latest tennis gear, as I did that day at the Masons, but I knew they were all going to be in for a shock when I commenced the game, as my chief fault was and is a complete inability to run for the ball.

The game began, and the other three threw themselves into the affray with all the fervour of Wimbledon champions, but it became increasingly obvious to them and the spectators that I was doing Kirk no good at all as his partner, and he became rather annoyed.

'Run for the ball, Diana,' he shouted desperately totally unaware that this was my big hang-up regarding the wretched game.

'Why didn't you run for the ball,' he kept snarling, gritting those famous teeth (the way he does on screen) and ferociously sucking in great gulps of air.

The ordeal finally came to a halt, with Ginger and James scoring a fantastic triumph, and Kirk looking sullen as he stalked off the court. He had every reason to be cross, but I suspected he was probably not a very good loser at the best of times, so enthusiastic was he about playing tennis.

Much to my relief I was not asked to play again that day, or for that matter ever again. This was probably how my friendship with Pamela got started, as she never played, and we used to sit gossiping, our favourite past-time!

Kirk must have forgiven me for, years later when I was living in Hollywood with my second husband and two children, Pam threw a birthday party in my honour, and one of the surprise guests she had invited was Kirk. He came alone and oozed charm the entire evening, so I figured he must have completely forgotten our abortive tennis partnership.

'Please do me a favour, Diana?' he asked during the party. 'Don't become good friends with my wife. They all do, and it ruins my relationships with women.'

I did not know quite how to take this and hoped he

did not mean what I thought he meant, but shrugged the subject off as merely the evening's *joie de vivre* and the effect of Pam's champagne!

At around eleven o'clock he excused himself by saying that he had to return home. I suspected his wife was probably due to telephone but he did not say this, of course, preferring to go out in true Kirk Douglas style, as he does at the end of all his marvellous movies.

'Do me another favour,' he said, gallantly kissing my hand and edging towards the door. 'When midnight strikes, I shall be lying in my bed all alone and thinking of you. Please think about me too!'

Sadly the party got rather hectic after his departure and, like Cinderella, I forgot the time until it was too late. To this day I wonder what Kirk Douglas was thinking about all alone in his king-sized bed at midnight.

## D is for DRACULA

If you think Dracula as portrayed by Vincent Price and Christopher Lee is pretty horrible he was nothing compared with the real one.
Vladimir Dracula lived many hundreds of years ago. Amongst his other activities he would often stab and skewer people then hang them above the dinner table.

One night a guest made the grave mistake of saying that the stench of dead bodies was spoiling his meal. Dracula promptly skewered him and hung him up with the others.

## D is for DRAG ARTISTS

I know they are very popular. Danny La Rue is one of the best loved entertainers in this country today, but I often find myself wondering what it must be like for the mother of these men to see their sons prancing about dressed up as women.

As a mother myself I don't think I would feel too

comfortable if one of my sons started appearing in drag, however.

Frankie Vaughan's son has decided to launch himself as a drag artist and happily Frankie and his wife Stella have accepted it all in good part.

I think women seem to be more amused by drag artists than men. In all women there is this fascination at seeing a man dressed up, looking better than most women and getting away with it.

Dustin Hoffman had gread success when he dressed up as a woman in the film *Tootsie*, having modelled his character on his mother.

The film was a box office success and had hundreds of American men also dressing up as women, competing in Tootsie lookalike contests. The mind boggles.

## D is for DRIVERS

Have you noticed how a man's personality changes the minute he gets behind a wheel? Suddenly, he can change into a raving maniac! Women should remember – there are two areas where you must never criticize a man: his driving and his prowess in bed.

## D is for DRUG ADDICTS

Drug addiction is a disease of our times. It is not only hell for the addict, but is extremely painful and sad for his loved ones. These days there are quite a lot of centres where addicts can get help – and their families can get support – but it is a long and often hopeless business.

Occasionally you hear of someone who has beaten the habit and, thankfully, people like my great friend comedian Freddie Starr who have the guts to tell their horrific stories of drug addiction give great aid to others.

Freddie was lucky. His family stuck by him. He had

a great career waiting for him and he managed to fight back.

I know he hopes that many young people will read about his addiction and have been turned off drugs forever.

## D is for DUELLISTS

Why do men try to blow each other's brains out over a woman? True, it is immensely flattering for a girl if she has two suitors arguing over her attention. But duelling at dawn seems a pretty silly and dangerous way to sort it out. Thankfully this type of settling who wins the fair maiden went out a good many years ago.

## D is for DUTCHMEN

A Dutchman named Rudy, with whom I appeared on television in Holland, once said, 'Speaking Dutch sounds like a disease of the throat!' Oh, and by the way, if you are female watch out for these men. The legendary story of Hans, the boy who sat with his finger in the dyke for hours on end, should be a warning to us all!

A-Z. M.—3

# E

*E is for EARLS*
The most notorious earl that springs to my mind was the uncle of the ill-fated Anne Boleyn, namely the Earl of Norfolk, who actually sat in court as a judge at her mock trial and helped send her to the execution block. If he did such a thing to his own niece, what chance did other members of the female sex have during his lifetime?

A present-day earl I have always liked is handsome Patrick Lichfield, cousin of the Queen Mother, photographer extraordinaire, and a man who once cashed in on his title by opening a shop for men called 'The Belted Earl' . . . However, I wonder what Britt Ekland's opinion was about him, in *her* book as a lover?

*E is for CLINT EASTWOOD*
A marvellous actor, a talented director and a rat! I don't think much of a man who having been married for many, many years to the same long-suffering wife who stood by him through the bad days suddenly drops her for a young actress appearing in one of his films.

Perhaps he woke up one day and thought, 'Good Heavens, Mrs Eastwood isn't looking too good any more.' Think about it, Clint, maybe the reason for that was because she had to live with *you* during those hard times when you were a struggling stunt man.

*E is for EGOTISTS (or the Famous Male Ego)*

Vanity and conceit in a woman is bad enough, but in the case of some ladies they can be forgiven, for what else have they got to think about? But the ego which never ceases to amaze me is that of the male!

Man's conceit over his prowess in pursuing and catching women has been going on since time began.

Very early on in any girl's life she is subjected to being chased by a man. Perhaps he takes her out to dinner, if he has the money, or maybe it is just a trip to the cinema with a packet of sweets thrown in, but at the end of the evening not only does he expect, he demands, kissing, canoodling or often a great deal more! Many a good evening out has been spoilt for a girl by the thought of the struggle which must inevitably ensue on the way home in the taxi, or at her front door, and all because the male ego considers he is utterly irresistible!

His amazement, and downright angry reaction to her refusal knows no bounds, and it has always seemed to me so wrongly taken for granted on the man's part! Happily I am not the only one who thinks this way, and it was finally brought home to me by a very experienced woman friend of mine who said, 'Always remember, if you say "no" and mean it, never feel guilty about the rejected suitor. If they've got the cheek to demand it in the first place, then you certainly have the cheek to refuse!'

My final point about the male ego is proven by the fact that ex-film actor Ronald Reagan (mentioned at length further on in this book) once decided to commemorate his wedding anniversary celebrations by having an enormous portrait of HIMSELF spun in sugar on top of the wedding cake.

Needless to say his wife Nancy did not feature at all!

*E is for ELVIS*
There was only one, so it is unnecessary to add Presley.

If any man was born with everything it takes to become a superstar in the way of looks, talent and sex appeal, Elvis had the proverbial silver spoon in his mouth.

He also managed to put a great deal more in that same mouth, which had rocked and shaken us all with a whole new concept of music way back in the fabulous fifties – and I do not just mean an assortment of junk food that would give most of us a heart attack.

How tragic that the once handsome face blew up like a balloon along with the rest of his body, due to a daily overdose of pills and drugs.

*E is for EMBROIDERERS*
Don't laugh! Some men actually do embroidery work, and just to prove my point, those two one-time Hollywood 'super-studs' Rock Hudson and Van Johnson, bachelors both, are sewing away quite happily to this day, wherever they happen to be living or working.

Years ago in this country there was a fervent embroiderer in the shape of actor Ernest Thesiger, who was also a confirmed bachelor, (odd how unmarried men take up this hobby) and his love of using the needle took him to Buckingham Palace, where he sewed tapestries with the late Queen Mary on many afternoons.

How do I know this to be true?

Ernest and I worked on a film together once, and he showed me the pearly necklace Queen Mary gave him as a little gift to show her appreciation of his company. He always wore it under his stiff wing collar.

*E is for DICK EMERY*

Dick couldn't resist a showgirl and said so himself many times. When the final curtain went up he had already picked out a new bed-mate and the affair lasted until the curtain came down for the last time.

Married five times and with many affairs behind him, he was incredibly sexy and had no trouble pulling young attractive women.

Dick also lived life to the full – fast cars, a magnificent home and his own aeroplane – but despite these things, a great insecurity made him try everything, including psychiatrists and hypnotists, to overcome his inferiority complex.

Even after his death the controversy that surrounded this talented comedian raged on – primarily there was the hassle over Dick's money. He left the bulk of his cash to Fay, his last mistress so naturally his wife Josephone demanded her share. She also sent a messenger to collect his ashes which Fay kept in her front room. I can now reveal that Dick wanted his remains scattered in the Thames but the powers that be prevented it because it was considered a health risk!

*E is for EMPERORS*

Emperors are thought of as dignified personages and possibly there have been a few Oriental ones, whose names escape me for the moment.

But if the notorious Tiberius, and his nephew Caligula, were anything to go by, then thankfully such Emperors do not exist anywhere, least of all in Rome, today.

It is hard to imagine such terrible acts of debauchery as these two managed to get up to in their leisure hours being performed by any member of the human race. Suffice it to say that throwing Christians to the lions became as boring to them as a vicarage tea-party, compared with some of their other exploits. Tiberius murdered his mother, and Caligula ripped his pregnant sister's child from the womb (which incidentally was his) and consumed it with relish!

*E is for ENGLISHMEN*
I have not been too kind to men so far in this book, particularly when it comes to their prowess as husbands. However, I personally think if a woman feels compelled to get married, then, providing they are not total male chauvinists, Englishmen make the best ones!

# F

*F is for* FAIRIES

You know that saying about fairies at the bottom of the garden? Are there any at the bottom of yours? I've certainly got two at the end of mine!

*F is for* FANTASIZERS

Most men are fantasizers when it comes to sex. Naturally women fantasize too but this is a book about the opposite sex. Therefore I am writing about men.

When I say men fantasize, I do not necessarily mean that the male needs to imagine he is making love to someone else when he is with his wife, but simply that they often have a fantasy female figure in mind during the whole of their lifetime.

This could be a young girl they may have fallen in love with in puberty, who was perhaps someone they might never have spoken to, but gazed at from afar. Sometimes a man's fantasy is the type of woman he actually goes for and marries – but this is really quite rare.

There are 'girlie' magazines which excite many men, but the most popular kind of fantasizing over the female form divine is the adoration of a 'screen goddess'. Today that 'goddess' is Bo Derek, but in the days before television or video, when going to the cinema was one of the highlights of pleasure and entertainment, film makers provided the public with hundreds of beautiful women, some of whom were good actresses, but by and large just glamorous objects for men to ogle.

Hollywood started the idea of making a handful of these women 'superstars', immortal women far beyond the reach of any man, except in his dreams; thus the platinum blonde Jean Harlow was born!

Following in her footsteps came Betty Grable, the GI's Pin-Up and main fantasy figure in World War Two, flanked by other 'goddesses' such as the 'omph' girl Ann Sheridan, Rita Hayworth, Lana Turner, Dorothy Lamour, Linda Darnell, Ava Gardner, Hedy Lamarr and Veronica Lake.

Finally came Marilyn Monroe, perhaps the greatest 'fantasy' screen goddess of them all, with France offering Brigitte Bardot as their figurehead, Italy boasting Gina Lollobrigida and Sophia Loren, and I have to say, proudly, England voted for me.

There were a few other blondes around in America who made men's pulses quicken, namely Doris Day, Jayne Mansfield and Kim Novak but it all came to an end with the collapse of the film industry in general, and men were left with only memories if they wished to fantasize about their particular 'dream girls'.

The point I am really making is that although the masculine public still held their fantasies intact, the women who provided them with those thrills, fared rather badly in real life when the passing of time made even 'goddesses' old and suddenly it seemed they were really only human after all!

Much of these females' misfortune throughout the years was of course of their own making but, as is the way with most women who allow their hearts to rule their heads, it was usually MEN who were the cause of the unhappiness they endured.

Let us look at the track records of those mentioned.

Jean Harlow was first married to a man who could not consummate the union and who committed suicide after the 'honeymoon'! Because of the over-sexed behaviour of her step-father, a lustful Italian, Jean

56

became frightened of sex, even though on screen she was America's top sex-symbol. She died at the tender age of twenty-six, having never really experienced the pleasures of love, marriage or motherhood.

Betty Grable, married and divorced from the once lovable child actor Jackie Coogan, star of *The Kid*, had an ill-fated love affair with gangster actor George Raft. After three years she grew tired of waiting for him to leave his wife, and married band-leader Harry James instead. The union, though regarded by the public as a happy one, resulted in divorce, due to James's thirst for other women and his physical violence towards her. Betty died, alone, from lung cancer.

Tragic Marilyn Monroe's love affairs and marriages to various men, including brilliant playwright Arthur Miller, have been written about so often it is unnecessary to elaborate on them. Suffice it to say that the mystery of her death is still unsolved, but it is no secret that she was having an affair with the late President Kennedy's brother Robert, who also refused to leave his wife for her.

In Europe, Bardot, Lollobrigida, Loren and I are still going strong, though not without having had a great deal of marital upheaval in our personal lives.

Doris Day's autobiography raised many eyebrows when the thrice-married star revealed ALL about herself, including two alcoholic husbands who physically abused her; the third left her with enormous debts to the income-tax man. Small wonder she now lives alone with just her dogs for company.

Jayne Mansfield, married five times, finally died in a horrific car smash with the lawyer with whom she was consorting, Sam Brody, a frightening man who not only physically abused her but did it in public for everyone to see. Ghastly photographs of Jayne, often very drunk, as she struggled to survive with such a man were frequently printed in newspapers before they both met their end on a motorway in Alabama.

Kim Novak was married twice. She had to endure a lot of public criticism when she had an affair with Sammy Davis Jnr because of racial prejudice, and again when Harry Cohn, head of Columbia Studios, gave her some large financial investments. Like Doris Day, she now lives alone on a remote part of the Californian coast.

Dorothy Lamour, Linda Darnell, Ann Sheridan and Hedy Lamarr totted up over a dozen childless marriages between them. Veronica Lake grew so depressed after three trips to the altar, law suits, having her children taken away, and struggles with her ex-husbands that she disappeared from Hollywood, had a nervous breakdown, and was finally discovered working as a cocktail waitress in New York, sipping more drinks than she served, before eventually dying.

The beautiful Ava Gardner married Mickey Rooney, Artie Shaw and Frank Sinatra, all turbulent unions which inevitably ended in divorce. Lana Turner married seven times, the last to a nightclub hypnotist named Ronald Dante who stole all her money. Between her fifth and sixth marriages she also encountered one Johnny Stompanato, a Mafia gangster who dominated her life and blacked her eyes so often that Lana's daughter Cheryl could stand witnessing no more and stabbed him to death with a kitchen carving knife.

It was left to the star of *Gilda*, the dream goddess of thousands of men everywhere, flame-haired Rita Hayworth, five times married and once to a prince, before alcohol and drugs forced a court judge to rule she had reached a stage of advanced senility (and placed her in care), to make the last statement regarding those who had married her and played out their fantasies. Rita said sadly, 'The problem about being a sex-goddess is that men go to bed with Gilda, and wake up with Rita Hayworth!'

## F is for FATHERS

A psychologist once told me that women are subconsciously looking for a father figure when they're choosing a husband. Well, I can tell you, my husband Alan is no father figure.

Who would want to be married to their dad? Having lived with him all through childhood, I'm sure most women go for the complete opposite, if only for a change! Meanwhile, I suppose we can all thank our lucky stars we did not have a father like American singer Connie Francis, who had her committed to a psychiatric home, because, he claimed, she spent too much money!

## F is for GUY FAWKES

What a strange country this is, where every year we still celebrate the horrific death of the man who tried to blow up the Houses of Parliament! America has its Independence Day which is worth celebrating but we burn Guy's effigy and gloat about the terrible torture that was inflicted on him.

I know he did wrong, but if we rejoice about such things maybe we should also celebrate events like Hitler's suicide in the bunker, or even have a 'Jack the Ripper' day down in Limehouse.

## F is for W. C. FIELDS

The incredible W. C. who, since his death, has probably been impersonated by almost every comedian in show-business.

Naturally I did not meet him, as he was before my time, but his reputation as a child- and animal-hater, together with all the other stories surrounding his life and career, have delighted me on many occasions.

Amongst many stories about W. C. Fields, there is one which typified his attitude to the studio bosses, and underlines how much money he was worth at the height of his career. He would get on a train and travel across country, alighting at obscure towns and opening bank deposit accounts to hide his vast fortune. To this day no one knows where all the accounts were, and indeed still are, hidden.

His behaviour at the zenith of his career is shown in an incident which happened whilst in the middle of filming. Apparently W. C. had found an alluring female friend, and decided to give work a miss for a while, so he took her, together with his valet, to some mountain retreat. Several days went by, and Jack Warner, the studio head, was going berserk, since the delay caused by the star's absence was making the already expensive film costs soar higher.

Desperately he telephoned the mountain chalet, pleading with the valet to persuade his master to return and finish the film, but the pleas fell on deaf ears, since W. C. would not even speak to him. Finally, frustrated with rage, he telephoned and issued the valet with an ultimatum. 'You tell that son of a bitch that if he is not back in my studio tomorrow morning to continue his movie, I will personally see to it that he never works in another studio or theatre anywhere in the world for the rest of his life . . . Now, go and tell him what Jack Warner has just said, and I'll hold on.'

The valet did as he was bid, and timidly opened the bedroom door saying, 'Mr Fields, it's Mr Warner on the phone. He says if you don't go back and finish the film, he will ruin you, not only in Hollywood but all over the world.'

There was a long pause as W. C. absorbed the threat.

'Well, what shall I tell him, sir? He's waiting on the telephone for your decision,' enquired the valet nervously . . .

'Give him an evasive answer,' drawled Fields in his inimitable way. 'Tell him to go and fuck himself!'

*F is for PETER FINCH*

The late hell-raising actor-rebel, who made history by winning an Oscar after his death. Finchy was a great character and I knew him well. We laughed together on many an occasion, and he cried on my shoulder one night when a love affair with a dusky English songstress had gone wrong. Whatever he did and wherever he went there was always fun and excitement. He rebelled against officialdom, especially the star system which we were all expected to adhere to in the old days with the J. Arthur Rank Organization. On one memorable photograph call at Pinewood Studios, as we were all lined up to be photographed he insisted on shouting, 'Shit!' each time the cameraman tried to take a picture of us all looking as though we were happy to be Rank stars. And as I remember it, he deliberately shocked the producers and 'powers that be' that day, by refusing to go and visit the Gents toilet. Instead, he put out the log fire in the bar in his own way!

Despite all the wild man publicity, and the press ballyhoo about his private life, he was a splendid actor, and he will be missed greatly.

One of his best films was *The Trials of Oscar Wilde*, and each time I see it I cry.

His performance was so sensitive and moving. No doubt I will cry again when next I look at it, for now he has gone, and the world is an emptier place.


*F is for FLASHERS*

Can you honestly imagine a woman standing in a quiet country lane, on a river bank, or wherever these sort of men choose to expose themselves, wearing a dirty raincoat? I can't, and I'm taking Erica Roe's streak across the football field into consideration.

*F is for ERROL FLYNN*

Undoubtedly the most handsome, colourful character ever to hit Hollywood. His book, *My Wicked, Wicked Ways*, told of his early life which was even more interesting than after he became an actor.

The stories of his romances, experiences, and jokes are endless. He had a great love of life, but the end came through too much vodka, heroin, and womanizing.

To gaze at Errol Flynn on the silver screen in wonder was one thing, to become involved with him emotionally must have been something else! Among the many law suits brought against him during his lifetime were a couple of rape charges on different occasions that earned him the reputation amongst American Servicemen as a lady-killer, whilst the nickname 'in like Flynn' became almost a password in its day. Few knew then that his hatred for women had really stemmed from how much he hated his mother as a child.

His long-suffering wives one by one sued him for divorce, and at the wedding reception given for his last marriage, to Patrice Wymore, Errol was actually served with a paternity suit, a wedding present that can hardly have delighted the new Mrs Flynn.

Of the many jokes he played on others throughout his life, there was none worse than the macabre one played on him by a couple of his close friends (male of course).

Knowing that Flynn's idol was John Barrymore, they waited until the poor man died and was lying in state at the Hollywood mortuary, then bribed some official there to allow them to take the body, on the night of the funeral, up to Flynn's house on Mulholland Drive while he was out.

Carefully, they laid Barrymore in an armchair by the fire and then hid, awaiting Flynn's return.

Around 2 a.m. he walked in, well-inebriated, and

one can only marvel that his heart did not stop there and then in fright, as he perceived, through his drunken haze, the figure of that fine actor sitting in a relaxed way in his armchair! Perhaps it was the effect of his beloved vodka that preserved him from leaving this world earlier than he did – at a sadly early age.

## F is for FOOTBALLERS

I know there are millions of football fans in the world, many of them women, and indeed, footballers today do look and behave like pop stars. But for the life of me I cannot understand how or why three television channels should devote hours to showing the game, leaving those of us who are not enthusiasts utterly bored! more curious though, is how twenty-two grown men can get that excited over chasing a little ball!

## F is for BRUCE FORSYTH

In one of my previous books I related an hilariously funny story which involved Bruce, myself, another comedian named Kenny Earle, and a 'drag' artiste. It happened back in the sixties when we were all appearing in cabaret in Stockton. We played a joke on Bruce, who at the time thought it quite amusing.

I have known, liked, and respected him as a person and an artist for many years. He has been to my home often for parties or all kinds of meetings, so it was peculiar to say the least when one day on a plane to Paris, Bruce practically ignored my normal cheery greeting.

On the next occasion I saw him, at a Royal Command Variety performance, he deliberately slithered into a corridor when he saw me approaching. At this point I began making enquiries as to what was the matter. I asked his estranged wife Anthea whatever the problem could be? Surely, I reasoned, it was not the harmless tale I had told in my book!

Despite her marital differences with Bruce who had publicly branded her an adulteress, and irrespective of anything he might have done, Anthea tried to be loyal. She explained that my story made him look as if he might have been a homosexual, and this had genuinely upset him.

Obviously, I understood that such a thing would be very unpleasant. Certainly no sane person, including myself, could ever think it was true – especially when his first wife Penny had gone to great lengths in the press to prove otherwise, by relating highly intimate details of their married life together, which also involved a grand piano being thrown up and down stairs (though even with Bruce's masculinity I could never understand how that happened!).

Sadly, her revelations, along with the problems over Anthea, plus the appalling notices he had received for several years which toppled him from number one favourite in the British entertainment world, I reckoned had upset his reasoning, and caused him to overreact to my silly little story. I wondered what had happened to that marvellous sense of humour he once possessed? I wish I could say something nice about him now to make everything pleasant again, but frankly Bruce to my mind you have now become a pain in the arse!

## F is for FRENCHMEN

Frenchmen are a vain, conceited lot! I loathe their accent, and if I hear Yves Montand state publicly once more that he gave Marilyn Monroe the 'elbow' when they made a film together entitled *Let's Make Love*, I will personally go to France and punch him on the nose!

*F is for DAVID FROST*
A man who has always appeared to have been lucky in business but, until his recent marriage, unlucky in love, which makes one wonder if he was good in the boardroom but not in the bedroom?

# G

*G is for CLARK GABLE*

It is unkind to speak ill of the dead, since obviously they cannot answer back, but everyone is entitled to their own opinion and as this book is all about men, I have to include the legendary King of Hollywood amongst my findings.

Here, in every woman's eyes, was a man, equalled by none in looks, sex appeal, charisma, and masculinity. When he swept Vivien Leigh off her feet and up that staircase in *Gone With The Wind* (the only good film he ever made by the way) there was not a dry seat in the cinema! Women's pulses raced, and there was not one female in the entire world who did not look at their husband or lover without thinking he had to be inferior to the great Gable.

As I have so often said before, fantasy is the basis for all sex, and if ever fantasy played its part in creating an image of the perfect man, other than Valentino, this was the time it happened.

The facts were that as an actor Gable was very mediocre, as a lover he may have been all right if a woman did not crave any sort of intelligent conversation afterwards, and as a husband he left much to be desired, as several of his ex-wives whom he used on his ambitious climb up the ladder of stardom, testified.

One of his leading ladies, Ava Gardner, summed the man up to an excited female fan one day when asked if Clark Gable's personality was really as stimulating as it appeared to be.

'Well,' she said after a few moment's thought, 'he

was the kind of guy who, if you said "Good morning! How are you?" He'd be stuck for an answer'!

*G is for GAMBLERS*

Probably a worse illness than alcoholism if that is possible, but, unlike that particular disease, it seems to affect men more than women.

God help the woman who is married to a gambler, for where with drink or drugs there is a limit to how much the victim needs before they are satisfied, or collapse, with gambling there is no end.

The bad Lord Byron, irresistible as he was to women, lost his entire fortune, home and goods on the turn of a card, and there have been thousands like him since who have lost their wives and families in the same manner, though today horses and dogs are the most popular ways to throw your money away.

Of course, with the advent of gaming casinos here in England many men spend most of their lives, and all the money they do not have, staring at a little ball spinning round on a roulette wheel in frantic antici-pation that if it drops into the right hole it will be the answer to all the problems they have created through their desire to flirt with danger.

I have known many gamblers. Not the least was a musical director at the Desert Inn at Las Vegas (aptly named Lost Wages!) who had gambled his whole life, and owed so much money around that terrifying town that he was forced to work for a set salary per week at the Desert Inn for the rest of his life. He was simply allowed enough to live quite frugally on a small part of his wages, whilst the rest paid back his 'markers' as they are so called all over the place.

A well-known British singer gambled and lost so much, including his wife, that he could no longer tour the country doing the only thing he knew, namely his nightclub act, for fear of being lynched by debtors. Consequently, he faded into bankruptcy and oblivion.

But the worst story was that of a man who was helplessly addicted to gambling. His wife, who had suffered untold misery through his addiction, was given a sum of money to use for the housekeeping for herself and the baby, and instructed NEVER to give in to his demands under any circumstances. When she refused adamantly, as she had been told, to give him any money, the husband snatched the baby from her arms and threatened to throw it on to the fire if she did not give him the necessary money for his 'unbeatable' horse. He lost, she lost, and the baby lost a father when they divorced.

## G is for GEMINI

The most irritating sign of the zodiac for Scorpios like myself. Heaven help any woman married to one of these, for as the Gemini man never knows which twin he is on certain days, how the hell can his poor unfortunate wife figure him out!

## G is for GENTLEMEN

'Always beware of "officers and gentlemen",' said an old homosexual to me once.

Do women really like 'gentlemen'? I often wonder!

## G is for RICHARD GERE

He has been hailed as the new Valentino but he acts like Greta Garbo. Since he shot to fame in the films *yanks* and *An Officer and a Gentleman*, Richard Gere has been Hollywood's hottest property. Everyone wants an interview with this handsome hunk to see if there's more to him than just good looks, but Mr Gere is saying nothing. He did once reluctantly consent to an interview with the staid *Ladies' Home Journal* but the reporter's first question was to ask him what it felt like to be a sex symbol. Gere replied by dropping his trousers. The reporter fled, the magazine didn't print the story and Gere to date has never given another interview.

## G is for JACKIE GLEASON

The American comedian who gave such a wonderful performance as Minnesota Fats in *The Hustler* with Paul Newman, for which he was nominated for an Oscar. Of all the branches of entertainment business I think comedy is the hardest, and if comedians have the capacity to make people laugh they can certainly make them cry; it is much more difficult.

To leave Jackie and his fellow comedians for a moment, however, I have three sons and although the eldest, Mark, is the image of me to look at, it is rather and embarrassing fact that the other two, Gary and Jason, look incredibly like two actors I have met once and only briefly. Jason particularly with his enormous blue eyes, could easily be the offspring of actor Malcolm MacDowell, especially when he pulls some of his wistful expressions – but I was only introduced to Malcolm at a restaurant in London one evening, so there was hardly a chance of consummating the association on that occasion. Gary, when he was two years old, looked unbelievably like Albert Finney who had just scored such a success with the film *Tom Jones*. Wherever I took him in Hollywood elderly matrons would point fingers at him and gushingly squeal, 'Oh Gee, it's Albert Finney!' I had never even met Albert at that point and did not do so until years later when introduced by my husband Alan who had filmed *Charlie Bubbles* with him. But back to Jackie Gleason and the birth of Gary at the Cedars of Lebanon Hospital in 1962. When you leave a hospital in Hollywood, especially after having a baby, a great fuss is made and you are wheeled right to your waiting car. Naturally, as I left with baby Gary wrapped in a blue shawl, television newsmen and press gathered around taking our pictures. 'Who do you think he looks like?' they asked, and as Gary was an enormous baby – he weighed 10 lbs 2 oz at birth and had a very round face surrounded by a mop of black hair – I gaily quipped, 'Jackie Gleason!' This was of course duly screened that night on television and the next day a telegram arrived at my Beverly Hills home addressed to Richard Dawson, my husband at that time. It read 'There are more reasons than one why that child looks like me. My regards to Miss Fluck. Signed Jackie Gleason.' We roared with laughter, but I was curious as to how he knew my maiden name. The answer was revealed later when I discovered he was filming at the time with a British actress and friend of mine, Glynis Johns, whom I had not seen since 1955 when we filmed *The Weak and the Wicked* together. She was at the bottom of it all – but to this day, I have still never met Mr Gleason.

*G is for GOEBBELS*

Hitler's propaganda minister and adviser, whose hold seems to have been as strong over his wife as it was over the Führer. This long-suffering soul bore him six or seven children whilst he wrote Hitler's dramatic speeches and spouted his mouth off to all and sundry!

In the last days in the bunker he advised Hitler and Eva Braun to commit suicide, but instead of doing the right thing by his wife and family, such as sending them away to the countryside, he insisted they all died too, so adamant was he that none of them could survive without him.

Maybe I ought to have listed him under E for supreme egotist!

## G is for GOLFERS
There is no way any woman can get one hundred per cent value out of this particular breed. And if you do not believe me, ask the thousands of golf widows, at this moment waiting for their fanatic partners to come home from the eighteenth – or nineteenth – hole!

## G is for GOLIATH
All I can say about this biblical giant is that he was the first man literally to be 'stoned from the start'!

## G is for GOSSIPERS
If you think this is a funny subject to have in a book about men, I have to state in my defence that I think men are far worse gossips than women. I can hear them all now protesting that they are not, but believe me they ARE.

Look in any office and there will usually be a gang of men having a good gossip. Down at the pub they pass on rumours quicker than girls ever could.

And why do you think it is that virtually all our newspaper gossip columnists are men? I think I've made my point!

## G is for GRANDFATHERS
Not all grandfathers are venerable old gentlemen, ready to play games with their children's children, or give them a shiny new fifty pence piece to put in their money-box (in my day it was half a crown if one was lucky).

Imagine starting life with Hermann Goering, Attila the Hun, or Ghengis Khan as a grandfather. Don't laugh – they all had grandchildren.

I do not think being the grandchild of a deposed President like Richard Nixon would be much fun either. Or for that matter, any other such man who had been found guilty of something and was beset by worries. Hardly the type to get down on all fours and play piggy-back with his small descendents if they wanted him to.

I never knew my two grandfathers, and from what I have been told I certainly did not miss much.

On my mother's side there were *two* men who qualified, it seemed. One was the man my grandmother married, and the other was his brother with whom she ran away, presumably unable to stand the boredom of life with her husband any longer.

This temptuous affair, which produced six more children besides the one she already had, sadly did not bring her the happiness she craved. Now I come to think of it, she would probably have been better off staying where she was when 'poverty came through the door, love went flying out of the window'. Years later the old devil left her for a bit of young stuff, the way men do, including grandfathers!

My father's father lived by strict Victorian standards. I suppose I cannot condemn him for that, particularly as Queen Victoria was on the throne. Judging by the photographs I saw he certainly did not fit the description of a jolly old Grandad.

Indeed, he was so far from jolly that, aside from running his home rather like the notorious Mr Barrett in *The Barretts of Wimpole Street*, he deliberately made his wife (my grandmother) pregnant after an argument, and then refused to speak to her during the following nine months for being so stupid as to allow herself to conceive!

All in all, I think my grandfathers were probably among the first of the male-chauvanists, and I hope there are not too many female readers who can say the same.

*G is for RUSSELL GRANT*

Breakfast Television's resident astrologer is really too
camp for words. However, he says it's nothing to do
with him. He really does get letters from Hull trawler-
men asking him to wave at them!

Camping it up nearly got Russell the sack from
Breakfast TV when he was first taking off. He'd made
some crack on the air about posing for photographs
and remarked, 'What is my best side? Some people
say my backside is all right.'

*G is for JOHN GREGSON*

The late actor – and a great friend for many years –
with whom I had the pleasure of working in several
films. Since I began writing this book so many famous
people, many of them friends of mine, have passed on.
It does not seem possible that they are not still around,
but if one has good memories they compensate a great
deal for the sadness and loss.

John had a wonderfully dry sense of humour, which
was just as well one night when I gave a party and he
came along quite unexpectedly to join in the fun. There
were many beautiful girls there but the one who took
John's eye was standing rather aloofly in the middle of
the room. I think someone had brought her in their
group as I did not really know who she was. John
asked me for an introduction but as I had not the
slightest idea of her name, I could not help him. 'Oh
just go on over and chat her up,' I said. Off he went,
only to return rather sadly, but still with the Gregson
humour overcoming the situation. It appears when he
made his bid for her attention the girl, much to his
surprise, for he was a pretty well-known actor, had
given him a rather cold reception and enquired haugh-
tily, 'What do you do?' This threw John considerably,
and he announced quietly that if that was the way
things were and the only girl he fancied in the room

73

did not even know of his existence, then the game was definitely up and so he might as well go home!

Actually, John was not the only star at the party who experienced a somewhat depressing encounter. Comedian Eric Sykes informed me that much to his chagrin, when he arrived a pretty girl had rushed up to him. Naturally he thought and hoped she fancied him! Sadly for Eric, the girl had merely been concerned about his welfare, and he felt about ninety-three when she asked politely, 'Mr Sykes would you like me to fetch you a chair?'

## G is for GROPERS

I have never met a female groper, but then I suppose the type of woman I know would not actually grope *me* even if she was that way inclined. I'm sure there are quite a few men who could relate stories of ladies whose hands perhaps rested a little too long on their thighs under the table during conversations. However, basically it is the male of the species, especially in Italy where groping is a national pastime, who are guilty of this self-indulgent and immature act.

Gropers in cinemas, or even the street, obviously derive some personal excitement as they quickly clutch at a part of the female anatomy, if only for a fleeting moment, although the idea of women running around behaving in the same manner is quite unthinkable (which is one of the reasons I maintain that we females are the superior sex!).

No, it is the man who takes a girl out on a date and has his hand up her skirt even before dinner who really offends me. How *dare* they think that she wants to be man-handled in such a disrespectful way.

All women love a caveman type, but I wonder if the fumbling gropers of this world really know or care how infantile and silly they appear to members of the opposite sex.

74

*G is for GYNAECOLOGISTS*
These men work where other men play . . . so what
arouses a gynaecologist sexually when he gets home at
night?

I should imagine it has to be an amazingly sensuous
woman, with a good many new ideas about variations
on an old theme! Thankfully I've never known a
gynaecologist other than on a professional basis.

# H

*H is for HANDYMEN*

It is certainly nice to have a man who is handy around the house. It saves a lot of cash if he can do a few jobs himself but handymen can be the biggest bores of all.

They go to work on a Monday morning and before anyone has the chance to ask them what kind of a weekend they had they are talling tales of how they built a two-storey extension in two days, or how they relaid the drive in two hours.

When I was a child we had some neighbours and the husband was such a fanatical do-it-yourselfer that his wife never knew what job he was going to start on next.

She was a school teacher and once came home from work to find her husband had 'made a start on the kitchen' which meant there was a huge pile of rubble which she had to climb over every time she went to put the kettle on.

He had only just started that job, of course, when the weather turned fine so he went outside to build another garage, saying he would finish the kitchen when the weather got bad again. It took two winters before that poor woman could get to her stove without needing climbing tackle.

Some men find doing physical jobs around the house a great turn-on. I don't know why, but as soon as they get their tools out they fancy sex.

I had a friend once who told me every time her husband went to start a job that needed doing in the house, he suddenly felt randy! They had a house full of unfinished projects but a wonderful sex life.

*H is for HANGMEN*

I have only ever met one hangman in my life – and thankfully it was not on a professional basis.

Hangmen and executioners on the whole are not a jolly lot. Indeed, in days gone by their way of becoming 'jolly' was usually to get as drunk as possible before an execution, no doubt to give themselves courage to perform the deed at all. This was fine for them but not so good for the unfortunate victim as he, or she, waited while the axe was wielded above their heads and often brought down with such drunken but inaccurate force that their necks were literally hacked from their shoulders.

Henry VIII was aware of this situation to the extent that when he ordered his second wife, Anne Boleyn, to be beheaded, he brought over a Frenchman whose prowess with a sword was unsurpassed (because he took heads off with a nice clean cut) to do the job properly.

This method was eventually abolished, in England at least, in favour of execution by hanging. And so to the story of how I met the last public hangman this country ever had, Albert Pierrepoint.

Back in 1953 I was making a film in Manchester with the late comedian Frank Randle. One day he informed me that Pierrepoint, an old friend of his, would be coming to visit the set. 'Whatever you do,' he warned, 'say nothing to him about his occupation. He is very reticent about it and never wants to discuss the subject.'

I promised faithfully to keep my 'trap shut' (if you will pardon the pun!). Curbing my desire to see what this sinister figure looked like, I awaited his arrival at the studios with interest.

To my amazement, Frank Randle appeared with a

tubby little man wearing an ordinary suit, pork pie hat, loud hand-painted tie, and sporting a large cigar stump in his mouth. He looked more like a bookmaker than a hangman. With hindsight I realized he would hardly be likely to walk about wearing a black hood over his head!

I was introduced to Mr Pierrepoint who behaved in a loud, rather brash manner and, true to my word, I let him do all the talking without once referring to his occupation.

After filming had finished that day he invited Frank, my first husband Denis and I back to the pub he owned just outside Manchester. I do not know what sort of a pub I imagined in my mind, but it certainly was a surprise when we got there. Naturally, on the Oldham Road, I did not expect to see a pretty little place with roses round the door. What I *did* see was a sign swinging backwards and forwards in the wind and rain heralding a grim-looking building named Help The Poor Struggler.

This was the first of many minor shocks I was to experience, for when we got inside I saw it was more of a beer house than a pub. There were 'sick joke' notices pinned up everywhere 'No hanging round the bar' and so forth.

Once inside his own domain, Albert Pierrepoint became his real self, the customers treated him like loyal subjects, and his brash humour now knew no bounds. We were ceremonially ushered into the back parlour and introduced to his wife, a pleasant, mild little woman who, when eventually I asked her what it felt like to be the wife of the hangman, replied, 'Oh well, someone's got to do it haven't they?' as if resigned to her fate and strange status in life.

Albert played host with a vengeance, liberally pouring out beers for the men, all the time cracking corny jokes, and sometimes bursting into song. Suddenly, as if the curtain had lifted on stage, he began talking non-stop about his job, reeling off names of people he had 'topped' as he put it, and giving intimate details of how they went. Spurred on by excitement, he produced a large book of press cuttings about himself, and I realized as he flicked over the pages, revealing his various headlines, that he had an ego bigger than any film star.

Once we realized he wanted to talk about himself, we peppered him with questions. He showed us an incredible book which contained the names of all the people he had hanged, their ages, weights, length of the drop, and the crimes they had committed. 'I have been offered thirty-five thousand pounds for that book,' announced Albert proudly. 'Then why don't you sell it, get away from all this and go and live in the South of France?' I asked, all too late realizing my remark had offended him by suggesting that his beerhouse was not a particularly nice place.

'If I did that,' he said huffily, 'I would have to retire, and I'm not ready to retire yet.'

More pictures and press cuttings followed, this time connected with the Nuremberg trials, and it was evident that Albert had had his nose well put out of joint by the Americans who had apparently packed him off home to England, thinking they could hang the Nazi war criminals better themselves.

It seemed that the man who had been hired for the job had made such a hash of it that they were shamefacedly forced to recall Albert to finish off the work professionally. 'Hangman flies back,' screeched one newspaper headline which he proudly showed me, together with some pictures of Nazi corpses with their necks stretched like chickens.

'They hadn't got a clue how to do it,' announced Albert grandly. 'The rope they used you could have towed the *Queen Mary* with. I use a very fine one.'

He mimed the size and style of his apparatus with great pride.

Drawn like a snake to the charmer, I pursued my questions, horrified by his revelations.

When I asked him if people panicked as the moment came for them to die he grew rather irritated at my naivety, stating quite seriously, 'I go to the prison the day before, shake them by the hand and say, 'Now you know who I am, do as I say and you'll be quite all right.'''

He paused as if waiting for me to digest this scene, and then added, 'Yes, I've had some lovely letters from mothers, thanking me for taking care of their sons.'

Helplessly I turned to his wife hoping that somewhere in this dingy back parlour a ray of light would appear, and said flippantly, 'How does it feel to go out and buy the groceries on Christie?'

He was a notorious murderer awaiting execution at the time, and indeed Albert had already shown us the Home Office letter requesting his presence at Pentonville prison to carry out Christie's hanging, but she merely shrugged and smiled half-heartedly.

I asked the question because I had heard that the fee for a hanging was extremely small, only about fifteen pounds a time in those days.

Happily, that was the last time I ever saw him.


*H is for RICHARD HARRIS*

The actor, hell-raiser and drinker is one of the wildest, yet greatest, people in show-business today. Not only is he a damn good actor, but he gives the profession a bit of excitement – which is all too sadly lacking nowadays – in the same style as when show-business first began with rogues, vagabonds and strolling players. No doubt there are a few producers still reeling from the effects of having employed Richard, despite his enormous box-office appeal, for if, when on location, he suddenly decides to take off for pastures new then nothing and no one can stop him.

Like the great Robert Newton there are many stories about him, but for the moment I had better deal with the one I know best.

As Alan had never visited Rome (it has always been my favourite city, surpassing Paris by miles in my opinion) we decided to go there for a sort of second honeymoon. Excitedly, I told him all about the wonderful sights, the fountains, statues, and above all the beautiful church of Saint Peter's in the heart of the Vatican. We were also on the brink of becoming Catholics so he looked forward to seeing this particular place very much.

Having settled down after the first day, I rushed him at once to Saint Peter's, eager to show him the works of Michelangelo, and all the other magnificent paintings and sculptures there. We entered the building and the atmosphere which always prevails seeped through us and thrilled our spirits.

Just as we were quietly admiring the work of an artist, a loud voice rang out behind me, making me rock on my heels, 'Diana Dors, what the hell are you doing here?' Looking round, I saw Richard standing with a photographer and a reporter from an English newspaper. To this day I do not know why he was there. He is a Catholic of course, and was making statements about getting in to see the Pope, regarding the Northern Ireland problem. At the time I did not pay much attention and talked happily to him as we had not seen each other for quite a while. Richard's natural ebullience got the better of him however and the more we talked the more excited he became at seeing an old friend so far away from home. He was alone (by this, I mean with no girlfriend) and anxious to arrange a good night out on the town as he was leaving the next day. The reporter, always on the lookout for something good to send back to his paper, suddenly had the idea of photographing us in the confessional and duly sent the pictures to England. But his paper considered they might be a little offensive to Catholics, so they were never printed.

That night we all met up at Richard's hotel, and noted that his previous problem of having no girlfriend had been rectified, for in his suite were several Italian beauties waiting to be escorted around Rome. Where he had gathered them from I do not know, but finally we all left one in particular hanging on his arm. It was the sort of Roman night one dreams about. We dined by candle light in a thousand-year-old cellar, and the party became very lively as the hours rolled by. Richard and Alan, both fortified by the potent Italian wine, sparked electrically, singing and joking until four a.m. when we all reluctantly decided it was time to leave. Outside in the little cobblestone street, dawn was beginning to break but, undaunted by the hour, Alan and Richard continued their merry-making somewhat noisily. It culminated with Alan singing an operatic aria with all the strength and sound of Concorde landing and Richard giving full vocal support. As their voices rang round the little street square, a window opened and an angry Italian lady roused from her slumbers proceeded to rain down an avalanche of abuse at the singing duo. On seeing their apparent indifference to her plight, she disappeared and then re-appeared with a large bucket of something and threw it at them. Unluckily Richard's girlfriend was standing in a position where she received the full blast of the contents, but the two main culprits were quite untouched. I often wondered afterwards whether she thought it was really worth a night with Richard Harris, to be soaked by someone's slops!

## H is for RUSSELL HARTY

Russell and I get on swimmingly! He came down to do one of his chat shows in my home from the indoor swimming pool? It was a fantastic night, great fun.

Russell is one of those people who have made it to the top by hard work and will never change. There has been no silver spoon for him, and he appreciates everything that comes his way.

I've done so many chat shows with him that I often joke to him that people will start to talk about us. Actually, that turned out to be a case of many a true word spoken in jest.

Alan and I had had a fight one day, and when we do, which happily is not often it is usually bad. Our son Jason, then aged six, on seeing my sad expression, suddenly came up with the solution, 'I think you had better get a divorce, mummy. Don't worry, you could marry Russell Harty, he likes you.'

## H is for LAURENCE HARVEY

Laurence was one of those tragic 'nearly men' of showbusiness. Apart from the hugely successful *Room at the Top*, he is not remembered for many other films. Yet he was a dedicated, skilled actor who was always on the verge of doing something great but never quite made it.

## H is for HEN-PECKED HUSBANDS

A full-grown man prancing around the kitchen with a drying up cloth in his hand and an apron tied round his waist is not a pretty sight. That isn't to say I don't think men should help around the house. Indeed, it is very nice if they do assist their wives out with a few of the chores occasionally.

But I am all for the happy medium. A hen-pecked man who does nothing before checking with his wife is not respected by men or women alike.

Whenever I see a husband so obviously very much under female rule, I often think that one day the worm will turn as it did in the film of that name I made with the Two Ronnies – and if it happens, heaven help *all* men, hen-pecked or otherwise!

*He is for HENRY VIII*
The findings of popular history always indicate that this man was a wicked king. He was an athletic type of male compared with most of his tiny Tudor contemporaries, and a fairly good man's man in his youth.

Where women were concerned Henry was extremely unlucky and, I suspect, something of a romantic, for anyone who composed the song 'Greensleeves' could not have been all bad!

However, amongst his sins were the terrible crimes of attacking the Church of Rome, destroying English Catholic churches and being responsible for the deaths of hundreds who did not go along with his plan to divorce his wife Catherine of Aragon, also the mother of his child Mary, and marry his mistress Anne Boleyn.

He plunged through a succession of wives thereafter, and subsequently became riddled with syphilis. As far as a wife was concerned, this was not the sort of husband to plead the old excuse of 'having a headache' when he demanded his conjugal rights, for he would quickly see to it that one would soon have no head which *could* ache!

*H is for HITLER*
It is difficult to imagine anyone liking this mad dictator.

I suppose his mother loved him and, aside from English aristocrat Unity Mitford's crush on him which culminated in her attempted suicide after he showed her the door, there was of course Eva Braun. With his nastly little moustache, and short back and sides one cannot imagine any woman fancying such a man. It just goes to show there is someone for everyone in this world.

## H is for HOMOSEXUALS

The only thing I really have against homosexuals is that they have taken a perfectly good English word, 'Gay', and turned it into something that represents a man who desires to have sex with another man.

Some of my best friends are homosexuals – I refuse to call them 'gays' – and by and large they are an extremely clever, amusing crowd. But when I imagine them in the act of having sex together I'm afraid it does cast a somewhat dark shadow on my feelings towards the matter.

It is strange how times change. In days gone by to be a queer, pansy, fairy, nancy-boy or whatever name was applied to this breed of men (so perhaps it was only natural they called themselves 'gays') was considered a dreadful thing. The great Oscar Wilde was imprisoned for his homosexuality, and I am the first to voice my outrage that it was a terrible thing to do to such a brilliant man.

But nowadays it really is the fashionable thing to be effeminate, particularly on television where artists like John Inman and Larry Grayson have achieved fame and fortune merely by acting in the same humorous manner that homosexuals have done in private for decades.

On the other hand, it can of course be a dangerous game and career breaker, if the homosexual is a public face and carries out his perversion in the sordidness of a public toilet. That IS against the law, for it may corrupt youngsters and also, as someone – Oscar Wilde? – once said, 'Should not be done in the street as it frightens the horses'.

I could write at length about many virile movie stars,

politicians and even a Prime Minister, whose manly images were not what they appeared to be, but it would ruin so many women's fantasies that they are better left alone.

As for the famous Jeremy Thorpe/Norman Scott case, here was a situation where a likeable, attractive politician, with every chance of becoming Prime Minister of Great Britain, had his chances dashed after lurid reports in the press concerning homosexual charges against him made by Scott.

It remains for that sultry, sexy singing star Eartha Kitt to sum up the problem of homosexuals where women are concerned in her own inimitable way:

'When you hear about palimony, alimony, galimony and gayimony, you can never be sure who is coming into your life, and for what reason.

'It is very difficult to find a good man. I'm looking for an old-fashioned one who sends me roses before we go out on a date. The trouble is just when I think I'm going out with a real man, he rings his boyfriend!'

## H is for BOB HOPE

The reason I went to Hollywood in the first place was actually due to Hope. For many years he had, amongst many other pilgrimages to American servicemen all over the world, made Iceland his mark at Christmas time. When he went he would always take along a glamorous female star to help boost the boys' morale. He invited me on one occasion, but I was filming and could not go. So the next time he came to these shores, he requested that I appear on a big television show he was doing here for American viewing. It was the fifties and I was at the height of my career. Bob, being a shrewd judge of box office appeal and glamour, had a specially scripted sketch written for us plus a lot of comedy material which we did in a 'stand-up' routine. I recall the first meeting with him in his suite at the

Dorchester Hotel. There were no less than seventeen script-writers sitting there, all on his payroll, and ready to supply him with gags and jokes for every occasion.

The show was eventually seen in the States, and this was the very first time anyone there came to know of my existence. Monroe was at her zenith and, with Bob's help and nationwide publicity, everyone suddenly became aware of a British blonde, whom they naturally thought had merely aped Marilyn and was hoping for stardom by jumping on her wagon.

Bob had an agent who had worked for him during his entire career. He was an incredible old character named Louis Shurr, or Doc. Aside from looking rather like a garden gnome, he had an eye for the ladies. Doc wore a rubber girdle to keep his stomach in, was driven everywhere by a coloured chauffeur named Hopkins, who looked much more dignified than his boss, and had a gimmick which all Hollywood knew and chuckled about! It is a recognized thing for a man to give a girl a mink coat if he can afford it, or if the mood takes him, but Doc Shurr was different. He was a bachelor and knew hundreds of pretty girls, and whenever he would escort some starlet to a film première he would provide them with a fabulous mink coat, which he owned, just to wear for the evening – rather on the lines of Cinderella having to give her ball-gown back at midnight.

When I was pushed into my swimming-pool at the party mentioned earlier, Doc Shurr was unlucky enough to be standing next to me just at that moment and went under too. Later, Bob Hope quipped in one of the trade magazines, 'Doc Shurr has ordered his new formal party outfit for the season – white tie, goggles and snorkel!' The picture of me climbing out of the water was circulated all round the world, and Doc Shurr's head was just below me, looking like John the Baptist after Salome had finished with him.

Doc had negotiated my contract with RKO and arranged for me to go to Hollywood, so he and Bob felt quite responsible for me, as if I was their property, which was extremely nice. At once point before my star began to wane, there was a strong possibility that Bob and I were going to re-make some of the old Jean Harlow films – comedies like *Blonde Bombshell*. Sadly, plans fell by the wayside.

About this time I received, and stupidly turned down, the lead in a film entitled *The Girl Can't Help It*, thereby giving Jayne Mansfield her first crack at film stardom which she seized with both hands!

I did do another television spectacular with Bob however, and it was great. My old and undisputed favourite James Cagney was guesting on it too, and I am proud to say I have met and worked with him.

Bob's studio, Paramount, was just across the road from mine at RKO and he and my first husband Dennis Hamilton used to send jokes and messages back to each other all the time. I also visited his fantastic home in Bel Air, with its enormous trophy room full of awards and honours collected by Bob over the years. He was actually born in England, though he seems to be such a typical American. One day I said to him: 'What would have happened, I wonder, if your parents had not left Eltham and gone to live in the States?' 'Quite simple,' he quipped, 'I would have been the English Tommy Trinder.'

*H is for ENGLEBERT 'HUMPERDINK'*
I am of course writing about the singer who was given that name by his manager Gordon Mills, also the manager of Tom Jones, in a last-ditch attempt to put some life into his sagging career. It worked, and he acquired recognition at long last after years of going round working-men's clubs under the name of 'Gerry Dorsey' and getting nowhere.

'Engelbert', or 'Gerry' as his old friends still call him, and which he loathes, is a fine singer who actually started out with the christian name of 'Arnold' – but that's another story!

I have nothing against him as an entertainer. However, as a husband, quite aside from the odd paternity suit he has had thrown at him from time to time by ladies who claim to have dallied with him whilst on tour doing his nightclub act, it seems that the whole image of 'Englebert' and the vast financial success that goes with it has affected him to such a degree that he even makes his poor, long-suffering wife call him 'Engle' in the privacy of their home.

## H is for HUNTSMEN

I cannot understand the urge these men have to hunt and kill wild creatures, whether they be foxes, birds or other animals, although the only excuse for the latter if it can be termed an excuse, is the vast amounts of money their pelts bring in.

Neither can I understand the activities of the Queen's husband, Prince Philip, who indulges in hunting (and in his case it certainly is not for the money) and yet at the same time spends long trips abroad on behalf of the World Wifelife Fund. One act completely contradicts the other.

## H is for HUSBANDS

Any married woman knows what husbands are really like in the privacy of the marital home, so I do not need to expand their faults and failings. However, the one thing I *would* like to know is, whose fantasy was it that a woman finds a husband, and then lives 'happily ever after'?

# I

*I is for INCOME TAX MEN*
Ugh!

*I is for RICHARD INGRAMS*
This man's occupation is editing a dreadful magazine
called *Private Eye* which delights in smearing the names
of the famous with shocking stories and cruel observa-
tions.

Newspaper men pursuing stories are one thing. Cash-
ing in, sadistically and sarcastically, on the misfortunes
of others, thus causing them a great deal of suffering, is
quite another. It is well-known that Ingrams plays the
organ in church on Sundays. I cannot abide hypocrites
and all I can say is God help him when he arrives as the
Heavenly Gates. I wonder if he will justify his actions
with callous and cryptic stories then?

*G is for INNOCENTS*
Yes really, there are such men, and it has nothing to do
with 'I for Impotence'!

Perhaps one should refer to them as male virgins.
I'm not talking about young boys but, even in this day
and age there are, still innocent males around who
know nothing about sex.

I had a girlfriend who was a virgin when she married
(quite a unique state back in the Sixties) and whose
bridegroom was a virgin too. This was also quite
unique but certainly a situation which happened many
times before over the decades. The difference with this
pair was that, whilst the blushing bride lay nervously in

bed on their wedding night, he made no attempt to touch her. His innocent reluctance was understandable – but he still made no attempt to touch her over the next six years!

Needless to say, the marriage floundered to a complete halt, but so sure was the bride that the whole problem was her fault, despite help from doctors and psychiatrists, she had two nervous breakdowns.

After the divorce, in which HE would up with the house and furniture, he married again and this time overcame his nervous innocence, producing two children very quickly! Proving once again that things can always end happily for the man, though often to some poor woman's emotional and financial cost.

To prove my point further, it seems that the author of *Peter Pan*, J. M. Barrie, so abhorred sex that he never did consummate his marriage and retired into the fantasy of never-never land for the rest of his life.

*I is for INSURANCE SALESMEN*
Comedian Woody Allen said it, not me!

'There ARE worse things in life than death . . . Have you ever spent an evening with an insurance salesman?'

*I is for IRISHMEN*
I am not over-fond of Irishmen. Aside from the fact that most of them drink too much, the only two I knew who really rate a word in this book were both 'peculiar' to say the least.

One was a publican and ex-showman who used to balance motor bikes in his teeth to prove his great strength or drinking capacity (I never knew which). The other had himself buried outside the aforementioned Irishman's pub for sixty days to prove that he could stay down there that long – doing so I might add for the ridiculous bet of one hundred pounds.

*I is for JEREMY IRONS*
Not many people know that this sexy star of *Brideshead Revisited* and *The French Lieutenant's Woman* started out as a char and handyman with an agency called Domestics Unlimited. How come I was never lucky enough to get such a handsome home help?

*I is for JUDAS ISCARIOT*
I'm sure I'm in the minority, at least I *know* I am as far as my Catholic priest is concerned, but I've always felt rather sorry for Judas Iscariot. If, as the Bible tells us, it was all prophesied before Jesus arrived on this Earth, then inevitably Judas had to do what he did.

Full of remorse afterwards, Judas hanged himself. As we are told God is all-forgiving. I am hopeful that he has forgiven this poor wretch.

*I is for ITALIANS*
I think Mussolini put paid to the general belief held by many women that Italians were usually dark and handsome lovers!

It is also a well-known fact that Italians make appalling husbands, for it seems that the custom in their country is to take a mistress *immediately* they have married a suitable woman, and the wives just have to put up with it.

Back in the fifties, however, one Italian wife had the last laugh. She was married to Italy's biggest screen heart-throb of those days, Rossano Brazzi. Like the rest of his married compatriots, he played away from home at every available opportunity.

The difference here was that each time he did so she would demand an expensive present, like a diamond bracelet, be pushed underneath her bedroom door before letting him in again. The result was that she amassed a fortune over the years as his career, and sexual urge, gradually dwindled away.

# J

### M is for MICK JAGGER

The rubber-lipped pop singer, who looks as if he has been chiselled out of granite and whose lower lip is not unlike my own, was actually once quoted as saying in an article about him entitled 'Dr Jagger and Mr Hyde', 'We all want to have an affair with our mother, it's a turn-on'!

It may well be so for him, but I do not know another man, apart from Oedipus with his mother complex, who has the same desire. However, this is a book about men, and, as the saying goes, 'It takes all sorts to make a world'!

### J is for JOCKEYS

It has always struck me as rather odd and somewhat obscene that jockeys perfer, and indeed marry, extra-large ladies.

But to be fair, I suppose it *is* difficult for most of them to find a woman of the same size.

### J is for TOM JONES

Tom, the sexiest singer ever to come out of Wales! Actually, I preferred the early Tom Jones, for when we first met he was a simple, nice lad, not too much of an intellect, with a rather limited sense of humour, but a straightforward, natural person. Today when I see him in photographs with a big fat cigar stuck in his mouth and trying to look like a tycoon (he could never look like Lew Grade thank goodness) I find the image has tarnished a little, and the Jones's boy's sex appeal not as attractive as it was once.

My first confrontation with Tom was one night after a television show called *Ready Steady Go* back in 1964. We went extremely well together, and our obvious attraction for each other was very evident to the watching viewers. He had just made a big hit with the song 'It's Not Unusual' and was new and ready for all the fun and trappings that went with success. I had been in the business a good few years by then, but I knew a good thing when I saw it! And I had seen nothing like him ANYWHERE, not even in Hollywood where there are more gorgeous men to the square foot than any other place in the world. I invited him back to my London flat where I had organized a party.

There were two drawbacks to what could have been a fine romance. He was married, and although my second husband Dickie Dawson and I were separated, because I never liked being alone, I too was quite attached to a pop singer, who had not then made the big-time as Tom was about to do, but who watched me like a hawk all evening, thereby making matters rather difficult for both Tom and myself.

On several occasions afterwards I met Tom, and his wife Linda, a sweet Welsh girl who was, and still is, completely devoted to him, despite the many rumours of other romances that have occurred in his life, and the thousands of women who throw their knickers at him, on stage and off.

I became very fond of them both, and once again when party time rolled round at my house I invited them to come and have some fun.

During the evening whilst we were barbecuing, Tom followed me out on to the terrace. His eyes glowed in the firelight, and we stood looking at each other for quite a long time without speaking. 'Have you ever had the feeling everyone is staring at you?' I joked, as

94

I could see Linda through the big glass window looking a little bit lost and out of it. Tom did not even smile, but as I said earlier he was not gifted with a large sense of humour. We started to talk about his marriage and he explained a great deal to me that night which was and always will be private. At the end of it I said, 'It's a pity really Tom, we would have made a great couple.' 'I know,' he answered, 'but I should have been afraid to make love to you.'

'Good heavens, why?' I gasped, disbelievingly.

'Well you always treat me like a child,' he said, 'And I'd be frightened that you would laugh at me.'

It was suddenly obvious to me that my sense of humour and ability to laugh at almost anything had given one of the world's top sex symbols cold feet in the love department. For a long while I tried to become a more serious person, but a leopard never changes its spots, so they say, and I am still laughing to this day . . . not only about life, but also whenever I see the Jones boy swivelling his hips and pretending to be the Great Lover!

## J is for J. R.

When J. R. Ewing burst on to our screens in *Dallas* he was evil, ruthless and a pig. So what happened?

We loved him and begged for more. Larry Hagman couldn't believe his luck that such a swine had made him a superstar.

However what really frightens me is that there is a little bit of J. R. in every man walking this earth.

## J is for JUDGES

I have often wondered whether these sombre-looking gentlemen are ever influenced, when sentencing someone to a lengthy jail term, by what is happening in their private lives. But, hard as it is to imagine, judges

ARE men and do experience the same sort of domestic problems or emotions as anybody else.

The notorious Judge Jeffries, who suffered from scrofula, piles and assorted venereal diseases, was probably the most evil one in history, sparing no one. Regardless of how he was feeling when presiding over the court he never showed any mercy. Thankfully modern day judges are not as sadistically cruel.

Another long since deceased judge, was a Scotsman named Deacon Brodie. A fine, respected member of the community, but invented the trap-door system for hanging.

All of this would have been highly commendable if Mr Brodie had left it at that, but after putting his wig and gown away for the day, by night he ran a band of robbers who pillaged and murdered their way through the streets of Edinburgh and made him rich on the proceeds. Thankfully, he was eventually found out and finally swung off with the aid of his own hanging contraption!

Today English judges are not corrupt, but in America, providing one has plenty of money, many judges can be bought and bribed which is a chilling thought.

Even this can go wrong however. On one occasion a young lawyer working for the Mafia in Chicago had paid the judge a fat fee not to sentence his client and the judge (for reasons of his own) suddenly reneged on the deal in court. The lawyer was so angry he leapt up, called him 'a dirty rat fink' and punched him on the nose!

This sort of behaviour could never happen here, I am happy to say, but judges do sometimes worry me, especially when one hears of them sentencing a man to thirty years for robbing a train, and another to mere probation for throwing a baby against the wall and killing it, because its crying interfered with his television viewing.

Even Prime Minister Margaret Thatcher saw fit to attack one judge, thus causing an uproar in the House of Commons (but then it is mainly *men* who are sitting there), for letting a man who had twice raped a six-year-old girl walk free after only spending twenty-six days in jail.

Once on my television chat-show I interviewed Judge Melford Stevens, a man with an extremely hard reputation for handing out stiff sentences, and asked him about the murderess Ruth Ellis the last woman to be hanged in this country. She was hanged in 1955 for something the French describe as 'a crime of passion'.

'A charming lady,' he said, 'with impeccable manners, but she deserved to die for shooting her lover.' At the time he was acting as defending counsel!

'Does your mood in court depend on the fact that your wife may have over-cooked your boiled egg for breakfast?' I ventured to ask.

'I never eat boiled eggs!' he replied coldly.

A – Z. M. — 5

# K

*K is for KENNEDYS*
It is now a well-know fact that Jack Kennedy had
several mistresses during the time he was President of
the United States, including one very famous and
glamorous American film star.

Indeed, the reason he is reputed to have fallen out
with Frank Sinatra, who had done so much for the
Kennedy campaign, was because he decided to spend
a weekend with this actress in Palm Springs.

Instead of staying at Frank Sinatra's house as he
usually did, Kennedy opted for Bing Crosby's home as
a hideaway and Frank never forgave him.

His brother, Bobby Kennedy, also quite a ladies'
man, was linked with many beauties during his lifetime, including Marilyn Monroe.

In 1960, while I was appearing in Cabaret at Ciro's
nightclub in Hollywood, Bobby happened to be sitting
at the back with his date – as always a very glamorous
lady. They were so totally engrossed with each other
that at one point they slid under the table and consequently never saw the end of my act at all!

*K is for GENGHIZ KHAN*
Although he was completely ruthless, this terrible man
was immortalized by Orson Welles in a film called
*Genghiz Khan*. Even with Orson's shape, that was small
come-uppance for the things Genghiz Khan did!

## K is for EDDIE KID

This is the young man who makes a living riding his motorbike over rows of old buses, like Evil Knievel. Therefore I sympathized with his wife, Debbie Ash, who had to take second place to a machine, which may have been why their marriage sadly floundered.

## K is for KINGS

It takes one hell of a woman to topple a king from his throne! Some have been instrumental in starting their downfall on occasions, but the one woman who really seemed to 'have what it takes' to make a King behave and feel like a man instead of a sovereign was the plain, almost ugly, American Mrs Wallis Simpson, back in 1937.

To put men under your spell is one thing, but to be paid the supreme compliment of having the King of England abdicate his throne because he 'could not live without her' as he described the feeling, is really an achievement.

The entire business says much for Mrs Simpson, later to become the Duchess of Windsor, but not a great deal for Edward VIII.

It was a pity he had not been like one of his predecessors, Henry VIII who would, I am sure, have found a means, possibly not an honourable one but certainly a solution, whereby he could have had the pleasure of the lady without actually marrying her! Millions wondered why Edward saw fit to give up his throne and live in exile when he could have had everything he wanted at home. But looking at his old house, Fort Belvedere, may provide the key. It was an odd construction to say the least, surrounded by little toy cannons, which did seem to indicate that this particular King was really only *playing* at being one.

Whatever his reasoning, Edward has gone down in history as being weak-willed over a woman. Other

Kings, like his grandfather Edward VII, the former and rather naughty old Prince of Wales, had dozens of mistresses, including Lily Langtry.

George IV could not abide his wife Queen Caroline, particularly becase of her lack of hygiene, so he enjoyed himself on the side with Mrs Fitzherbert and others.

Henry II was a great womanizer who even locked his wife Eleanor away for ten years so that he could get on with his extra marital activities in peace.

Charles II had Nell Gwynn.

And we all know about Henry VIII!

So what went wrong with King Edward VIII?

I suppose it all goes to prove that in the final analysis, Kings are only men, and men are the same the world over!

*K is for KNIGHTS*

The fairy tale myth of the knight in shining armour who rescues the princess from the jaws of the dragon and carries her off on his white horse, has been well and truly exploded in this age we live in. Certainly many a poor unsuspecting female, including myself, weaned on the idea of finding her hero and living 'happily ever after' has suffered the experience of discovering that all this childhood propaganda was really a MYTH in the true sens of the word.

Probably the only knights of any consequence we are aware of are the knights of the theatre. This brings me immediately to my theory, and it is one shared by many fellow artistes, that actors should not be given titles, for we are all basically strolling players. Gypsies, vagabonds and, in some cases, thieves.

The late Henry Irving, the first actor to be knighted, was really to blame for starting it all. One of his contemporaries moaned bitterly at the time, 'Henry should never have accepted the knighthood, he has made us all respectable'. However, it has gone on from there, and now we have so many theatrical knights, it has become almost farcical!

It is, of course, a great honour, awarded presumably for an actor's ability to do what is only a job of work, and who is to say which selected few should be singled out from others who are all equally as good?

Perhaps I would not feel as strongly about it if the powers that be offered to make me a Dame, but God forbid the day will ever come. I would hate that title anyway, it reminds me of Old Mother Riley.

Dame Diana Dors has a pantomime ring to it and is not nearly as dignified as, say, Sir Michael Redgrave or, even more illustrious, Lord Oliver. I am not knocking any of the noble theatrical knights, neither am I undermining their talents, though I suspect that deep down beneath those lofty exteriors, there must lurk some very satisfied egos at being dubbed with a title above all the rest. However, who am I to say that the late Sir Ralph Richardson, and the living Sir John Mills, Sir Richard Attenborough and Sir Alec Guiness, do not warrant the odd curtsey as a result of their labours. The pleasure they must derive from their honours is probably summed up by the sweet little tale of Sir John Gielgud who was once placed in the terrible position of trying to board a bus in Sloane Square, no doubt after a performance at the Royal Court theatre where he has had so many triumphs.

Sadly, Sir John's judgement as to where the platform actually was seems to have been slightly impaired that day, and one of his noble feet got caught in a position which prevented him from either boarding or disembarking. In this undignified and dangerous state he was forcibly carried around the square, apparently to the indifference of the driver and passengers within, who, with all due respect, did not appear to even recognize him.

Thinking his end was in sight with, much worse,

101

not even a good round of applause to 'go out on', the poor man swallowed his pride and called out in frantic desperation, enunciating in the clear Shakespearian tones which had helped to earn him his Knighthood . . . 'Stop, stop. You are killing a *genius*!'

My final word on the subject of titles and Knighthoods for actors must be that I sincerely hope no-one will ever be misguided enough to bestow one on Rex Harrison. Such an honour could not happen to a nastier person!

# L

*L is for DANNY LA RUE*

Danny has been making a living out of dressing up as a woman for thirty-two years and good luck to him. He's a professional performer who is brilliant at what he does.

He tries desperately to make sure theatres don't charge too much for tickets at one of his shows because he'd rather have a full theatre paying £2 each than a half-empty theatre paying £4.

Danny is one of the few entertainers around today who can really pull the crowds, and I'm sure a good proportion of his audience are there in the hope of catching him out by spotting where he puts his private parts!

*L is for MARQUIS DE LAVALETTE*

This French nobleman was jailed for sending secret messages to Napoleon but if you think he rotted in some seedy cell you are wrong. His wife arrived and took his place, enabling the Marquis to go free.

It just goes to show that these Frenchmen must have something (though they never appealed to me – as you read under the letter *F*).

*L is for LAWYERS*

I do not like lawyers – but that is probably because I have had so many dealings with them, and it has always cost me a great deal of money at the end of the day.

One lawyer I knew who kidded himself he looked

103

like Laurence Olivier, and who wound up hanging himself in his own garage (not because I hadn't paid my bill, I hasten to add), was extremely charming where lady clients were concerned. The trouble was that as he escorted you to the lift from his office, bowed and kissed your hand as the gates closed, you knew an extra ten pounds was going to be put on the account.

There is a wise story concerning lawyers which everyone should remember. Two farmers were quarrelling over a cow. One farmer was pulling it by the horns and the other farmer was pulling it by the tail, each claiming it was his.

Whilst the lawyer was underneath getting all the milk!

## L is for LAZY MEN

I can't abide laziness in either men or women.

But I can think of nothing worse than a woman, as many do, having to get up early on a cold winter's morning and go to work leaving her man snoring between the sheets.

## L is for SIR RUPERT LEIGH

Some men react in the most strange ways when they discover their wife has been deceiving them. This eighteenth-century cuckold found out that his wife was running away with her lover so he gave chase. He found the lovers on top of a cliff. During the scuffle his beloved wife fell over the cliff top and her lover escaped.

Sir Rupert, bless his heart, climbed down the treacherous cliff side and managed to carry his wife to safety. But she remained crippled and disfigured for the rest of her life. Sir Rupert nursed her until she died and to this day the cliff in Devon that was the scene of such a tragic domestic dispute is called Rupert's Head.

It would seem that even though he kept his wife –

his life was just as miserable as if he had let her go. There must be a moral in there somewhere.

## L is for LEO
If you are the sort of woman who can live with this man roaring in your ear day and night, then by all means take him on, and good luck to you!

## L is for JERRY LEWIS
One of the zaniest and most brilliant comedians of all time in my opinion, and according to his box office receipts I was obviously not the only one who thought so. But sadly this comic genius is also possessed of a manic ego. He and I got off to a bad start. It was not my fault but his enormous ego working overtime.

I first met Jerry when he was partnering Dean Martin at their debut appearance in London at the Palladium way back in 1953, and then again some years later in 1958 when he and Dean had split up and he was working alone. Once more there were pictures taken of us together in the star dressing-room. Afterwards during conversation I first saw the big power complex at work. 'You see this?' he announced shoving a bell type contraption attached to a long wire at me. 'This is the Panic Button and when I press it everyone comes running 'cos they know the big chief wants a pow-wow!' I expressed my compliments on the electrical wizardry of the gadget, but felt secretly very glad that I was not working with him or under him in the show as I cannot bear the kind of sycophantic behaviour which goes on around a superstar, especially American ones who surround themselves with a retinue of people ready to bow and cater to their every whim. It reminds me of medieval days (not that I was there!) when the court circled round King Henry VIII. If he laughed they all broke into hysterics even when they did not understand the joke; but if he was not amused they all looked glum.

Our next meeting was to be much more significant. It was now 1960 in Hollywood and Jerry Lewis was making another of his highly successful films, this one called *The Ladies' Man*. He had expressed a desire to see me and my agent about a star role in the picture, so we presented ourselves at Paramount Studios to find the trademark of Jerry Lewis everywhere. Hal Wallis who used to run the studios had been put out of business by King Jerry, who still hated him for the days when Wallis used to hit his desk with a large whip, shouting, 'Be funny' at Jerry and Dean Martin. Jerry Lewis's name was everywhere – there were even little electric run-around trucks like golf course carriers painted pink, with drawings of him cartooned on the sides. I thought to myself, what a marvellous feeling of power it must be to have lifted himself up into that illustrious position after years of oppression and being kicked around!

We were ushered into the main block of offices and eventually taken into the holy of holies – namely his large office which of course had once been Hal Wallis's. There sat Jerry behind the desk (which Wallis had whacked so often during the days when Jerry and Dean had been hauled up in front of him for a lecture), and I also noted the window behind him where it is reported that Burt Lancaster once in a fit of uncontrollable anger, unable to stand any more tyranny from Wallis, had tried to strangle him and push him through.

Jerry was charm itself that afternoon, anxious to impress with all his gadgets and jokes and I noted that the Panic Button was still there too. When we finally got round to discussing a deal, he asked my agent, who was sitting timidly in the corner, what sort of money he wanted for my services. The agent gulped and asked what he was prepared to pay, at which Jerry looked stern and repeated his former question in a manner which Hal Wallis might have done.

'Er, well, as it's a small guest role,' began my agent, 'Perhaps you would agree to, well shall we say seven thousand dollars?' 'No, we will not,' said Jerry, 'I will definitely not pay that to Miss Dors.' 'Oh well,' drooled the agent nervously, 'then whatever you think is best.' 'You have not asked me why I will not pay seven thousand bucks yet,' came the reply. 'Oh well Mr Lewis, why not?' asked the now totally demolished agent. 'Because I think she is worth more than that and you are underselling her,' shouted Lewis, who was now squirming in his seat as he excitedly played the power game with the grovelling man in the corner. 'I will pay her ten thousand dollars,' he announced striking the desk with his fist, and looking as though he wished he had a whip in the drawer. My agent's face was a study – the poor man was utterly wiped out with the situation, but a deal was done and we left the studio, confused but happy.

The film was due to commence a month or two later, and during the interim period an offer was made for me to appear with comedian Danny Kaye in a film he was making, *At the Double*. There were a great many British stars in it as the action was mainly supposed to be in England, so I was a natural for the part. I completed my work with Danny and then sat back and waited for my call to begin Jerry's film. Time went by and no call came. The movie started and I had not even received a call from Edith Head, the wardrobe designer, to discuss my costume. I began to worry as to what was going on and my agent proceeded to negotiate with the Lewis Production office as to what was happening.

We eventually learned to our amazement that Jerry had gone into a fit of jealousy because I had done the

107

picture with Danny Kaye first. I suppose he looked upon him as a rival – though I find it hard to believe with his enormous ego that he ever truly regarded anyone as that!

Harsh words were exchanged between the studios and my agents. We had a contract and it held good, so whether I appeared in the film or not, I had to be paid! One day I suddenly received a call to be at the studios the next morning at seven a.m. I duly presented myself in the make-up and hairdressing departments, who all expressed great surprise to see me as my name was not on the callsheet. As they were unable to do anything to me, I went and sat in a dressing-room trailer on the set, and waited. It was a very strange situation. Other actors I knew who were working on the film kept coming in and saying, 'What are you doing here?' The camera crew also nodded welcomes, but I was just left sitting in there all morning, rather like a prisoner waiting in the cells under the court for his time to come to go into the witness box.

At one point during the morning I saw Jerry go by, with not a glance at me although he obviously knew I was there. I had seen no script so if I had been called on to the set I would not have known what to do.

Finally, as lunchtime drew near, the assistant director came into my trailer looking rather embarrassed and said, 'Mr Lewis has sent me to say he cannot stand it any longer, and that he is sorry he has treated another artiste this way – you are free to go home.' I left, was paid the money, but never appeared in the film and was told, as much as a year later, by a girl he knew that she thought it was terrible the way I had treated Jerry, and how sorry she felt for him.

I think the only occasion when he was actually stopped dead in his tracks was due to a very funny gag played on him by another comedian, Phil Silvers of Bilko fame. It seems, back at the beginning of their success, Martin and Lewis were playing the Copacabana club in New York and ripping it up every night. The Copa was situated on the ground floor of an enormous skyscraper building of apartments, and right at the very top, in his bachelor days, lived Phil Silvers. One night, around one a.m., as the comedy team were paralysing the audience, Phil could not sleep. So up he got, put a dressing gown over his pyjamas and went down in his private lift some twenty floors below to ground level where the Copa was. Without any warning he marched straight into the club and on to the nightclub floor, much to the amazement of the audience, grabbed the microphone, and said 'Keep it down will you fellows, I'm trying to get some sleep,' walked right off the floor and into his lift leaving the audience, and Martin and Lewis, completely dumbfounded.

## L is for LIARS

A liar, man or woman, is a loathsome thing.

The worst one I knew was a man of course. His lying was so pathological that if he told you it was raining outside, you knew without turning your face to the window that it was probably quite a pleasant sunny day.

I could fill a book with stories of his lies and the escapades in which he became involved as a result, but the most blatantly successful lie of all occurred during a trip we made with some others to a hotel in Birmingham.

Having organized the various suites we were all to occupy, he ensconced himself in the best one with a young lady who was not his wife, issuing instructions to the hall porter that he was not to be disturbed under any circumstances.

Half-way through the night his wife arrived at the hotel, and demanded to be shown to her husband's room. The porter rang him to ask what he should do and was told very brusquely that he was NOT to disturb him again, and that she must wait downstairs until a respectable time in the morning.

As the poor woman could not go round knocking on every door in that large hotel trying to find him, she was forced to sit in the lobby all night. Finally, at 9 a.m. she informed the porter that she was on her way up, having by then found out his room number.

There was a terrible panic when the porter informed him of the situation rapidly bearing down upon him, but he managed to get rid of the lady with whom he had spent the night in the service elevator before his wife alighted from the other one and marched into his suite.

'How will he ever manage to explain his extraordinary behaviour to her, let alone the fact that he is here *at all*,' I wondered, but once again his competence as a liar overcame everything.

Five minutes later, she emerged, tears streaming down her face.

'What happened?' I ventured to ask.

In a voice choked with emotion she replied, 'He has told me everything.'

'EVERYTHING?' I gasped, unable to believe that for the first time in his life he had spoken the truth, particularly after keeping her waiting downstairs all night while he made love to another woman upstairs.

'He found out yesterday he has terminal cancer, and is going to die in six months,' she sobbed.

Unfortunately, I cannot complete the story as after that I lost touch with him. I do not know what lies he told when the six months were up, but with *his* prowess for lying I am sure he thought of something!

Of course any man can lie but some do it more convincingly than others. Eyes and hands can be a giveaway but most prolific fibbers know about that so they learn to lie with their eyes as well.

110

However, the next time you suspect someone of lying to you, look at his . . . FEET. I know it sounds silly but researchers have proved that liars can control other parts of their body but generally forget about their feet.

A liar is never able to stand still. He will change his weight from one foot to the other. Hence the expression: a shifty character –!

## L is for LIBERACE

Let me say straight away that anyone saying anything against this highly professional star regarding his public or personal life, will be in danger of having to deal with me as a result.

If someone is fortunate enough to know Lee, when the tinsel wrappings and gimmicks are swept away, then underneath they will find a genuine and unbelievably kind man. Though he revels in performing on stage, he rushes through life at break-neck speed, appearing wherever they will let him tickle the ivories. He is only truly happy when he is working but he also likes nothing better than staying at home with friends, eating and playing games. Now I am not trying to persuade my reader that lurking beneath Lee's extravagant exterior is a quiet soul who prefers a hermit's existence with pipe and slippers – quite the contrary – but he once confided to me that during his hectic and busy year of work, the two occasions he insists on being at home are Christmas and in May when the lilacs are blooming on his birthday.

When I went to Hollywood in 1956, I first met him at a rather smart but dull party, leaning against a wall looking somewhat sad. When I asked him what was wrong, I found out something which is a key to his real character. It seems that two nights before he had given a concert for charity in the Hollywood Bowl at the request of the *Los Angeles Times* who, after packing the place thanks to his name and making a great deal of money, had turned around and lambasted his performance the next day in their newspaper. This was of course a terrible thing to do, but where was the man who reputedly shrugged off all his critics with statements such as 'Let 'em knock, I laugh all the way to the bank'?

That night I realized he was only a human like the rest of us, and did care very deeply. When people attacked him it wounded him very much. I tried to boost his morale a little by telling him that when he came to England for the first time, which he was going to do a few weeks from then, the British press would love him, and so would the British public. It turned out I was wrong about the press, as secretly I feared I would be. During his first visit, despite the enormous success he enjoyed at the London Palladium and everywhere else he went, the press carved him up badly. One columnist, now deceased, saw fit to write the most scathing article ever written about anyone, criticizing his clothes, sex life, and many other private things. Lee created a precedent by suing this particular paper, much to the delight of all show-business people, for no one had ever dared to sue the press for fear of losing, and thus gaining bad publicity from all quarters. Lee not only sued, but won, although it cost him a fortune, much more than he was awarded. But he did it as a demand for respect and the truth despite the most horrible publicity any artiste was ever forced to receive as the trial unfolded, and the grisly facts were analysed over and over again in court.

I have known him closely for twenty-two years and he is a godfather to one of my sons, Gary. Of course his life-style is flamboyant, and there are many show people I know who sneer at me for being his friend. 'What's with that guy?' they say. 'How can anyone live the way he does with a piano-shaped swimming pool, and bed, plus all the pictures, trophies and trappings of his career spread out in rich splendour all over the house?' Well, the answer is that none of these things are really Lee. Yes, he revels in being Liberace and all the early homes and gimmicks were done for a purpose: to make him a millionaire, which he is today several times over. If the knockers were honest they would admit that they too would have done the same if they thought it would result in the kind of wealth and luxury Lee enjoys.

I have spent Christmas at his home, a showplace overlooking Hollywood which is now open to the public, and watched him open all his presents excitedly like a small boy, amidst the five Christmas trees all in different colours and lights decorating the drawing-room.

On my last visit to his beautiful, new and very private home in Palm Springs, Alan and I were treated like royalty, but then I suspect Lee lives better than royalty! The house, unlike all the others he has owned with their gimmicks and star-style decor, is so tastefully furnished and elegantly designed, it is fit for a prince. The dinner he held in our honour was second only to a meal one might expect at Maxims in Paris, with gold and silverware, crystal glasses, candle-light chandeliers, and superb cuisine. Typical of Lee, under each guest's plate, he placed a little gift which he had shopped for all day, and derived more pleasure in watching people's faces as they opened the packages, than ever he would have done if we had all brought gifts for him. He actually owns three other homes in Palm Springs; one which he bought, designed, and styled for his mother as a present which she refused to even go to see; and the other two just as 'fun' homes, as he describes them.

In the past Lee had a whale of a time dressing flamboyantly, and wearing outrageous clothes and jewels which, back in the fifties, created a great deal of excitement. But when the sixties began really swinging, and everyone freaked out with their clothes, Lee who was here on yet another tour, told me rather worriedly that he did not know what new gimmick to pull, as by then the public had seen everything. To use his words, 'I just cannot keep up with the game like I used to, there are so many "way out" clothes in the shops now, I've got to think of a different gimmick'. For several days he racked his brains as to what to give the audience on his opening night at the Palladium and finally announced that he was coming up with something special, but refused to reveal what it was to anybody including me.

The opening night arrived, and I sat in the audience waiting and wondering what he could do which had not already been done by countless, far-out rock groups and singers who were also much younger than him. As usual he went through his act, playing the piano, showing off his jewels and taking the mickey out of himself, while the audience cheered and applauded. His suit was glittering and styled in the usual fashion, and he also managed to get off and make a change, appearing in another suit of even more stunning proportions. Even s; I could not help thinking that all these things had been seen and done before, and he was really going to have to pull something big out of the bag to make the audience sit up this time.

Suddenly at the end of his show he did it, and once again the Liberace we had all come to know, and either love or despise, blossomed forth. Standing centre stage and taking his last bows graciously, I noted that he seemed to be holding one hand behind his back and wondered why . . . then it happened, unknown to us he was clutching a small electric box, complete with switch, and just as he was bowing for the last time, his entire suit lit up like one of the Christmas trees at his house in Hollywood. He was covered from head to foot in lights which had been sewn all over him for the occasion.

It was very spectacular and the audience went wild, but afterwards in the dressing-room he confided to me that it had been 'sink or swim' for he was in danger of blowing himself up in the process, and regardless of his desire to have a big finish, this was not the way Liberace truly wanted to go!

## L is for LIBRA
These men are sensitive and artistic it is true, but Libran males are the most argumentative in the zodiac. In their minds they are ALWAYS right, and they will continue to try and prove it long after you have collapsed from exhaustion.

## L is for 'LIVE-IN LOVERS'
If these spineless, self-styled 'live-in' lovers have not got the guts to ask a girl's hand in marriage, they're not worth the time a female wastes on them. I am not saying matrimony is the complete answer, but at least it is the supreme compliment a man can pay a woman if he *really* wants to live with her for the rest of his life.

## L is for 'RED KEN' LIVINGSTONE
Described as the Trotsky of County Hall, this Greater London Council leader is certainly the type of a man only a mother could love – but not the mothers of those murdered by the IRA.

Despite the horrors of the killings in Hyde Park and Regent's Park he still had the gall to invite the leaders of Sinn Fein over to Britain as his guests less than a year after the carnage.

*L is for LORDS*

Sadly, I was not around to experience the charms of the late Lord Byron. Despite his club foot, as a poet, gambler and womanizer, he seems to have been quite a man!

Many women fell under his spell including Lady Caroline Lamb, and his friend, the poet Shelley's wife. She incidentally, was the creator of Frankenstein and his monster, though I am sure she did not base the character on Byron.

I have known a few Lords in my time. In their favour I have to say that the saying 'drunk as a lord' never applied. However, their behaviour did not match up to their titles. One went to prison, another stripped naked and ran into my bedroom once at a house party in a frantic attempt to prove his virility, and one was fined for smuggling 'pot' out of the country after his wedding reception.

Another Lord, whom I did not know, was seated one evening at a table near mine in a restaurant. He proceeded to berate his Lady wife in a manner most unbecoming to his title. As their argument wore on and their voices (particularly his) grew louder and louder, the entire establishment heard Her Ladyship being accused of performing all sorts of sexual contortions on the kitchen floor with the footman and the butler – though whether they were all three supposed to have been doing it at the same time was somewhat unclear, due to His Lordship's rage! If it were true then of course he had good reason to be angry, but what puzzled me was why he chose a public place to have it out with her, if you will pardon the expression!

Lord Longford, otherwise known as Lord 'Porn' is also an acquaintance of mine, and one with whom I have worked professionally. Frank is a man who means well and whose heart is in the right place. His battle against pornography is tireless, but does come in for a great deal of ridicule from many quarters. One joke which circulated after he had completed an exhausting tour of Norway, Denmark and Sweden, was that 'His Lordship had actually scoured Scandinavia in a diligent search for an erection!'

## L is for LORRYDRIVERS

Other than the fact that I have two uncles who once worked as lorry-drivers, I do not know a great deal about this breed, except that like salesmen, they have a rather naughty reputation when it comes to playing away from home on the long working trips they are forced to make.

However, my knowledge of lorry-drivers was enhanced (if one can call it that) when, many years ago, I made a film about them entitled *The Long Haul*. My co-star on this well-forgotten epic was none other than one of Hollywood's super- super-studs at the time, Victor Mature.

As it happened, despite the appalling notices the film received we had a lot of laughs making it. Indeed, the movie also made a lot of money, which is comforting when one has been torn to shreds by the critics. One can 'laugh all the way to the bank' as Liberace so aptly put it while he counted his millions.

Victor Mature has been laughing all the way to the bank for most of his career.

He was the first person to admit that he could not act, and had only two expressions which he numbered 'five' and 'eight'. These involved using his eyebrows in upward and downward positions, thereby looking as though he was giving a sensitive and intelligent performance! In films like *Samson and Delilah*, and *The Robe*, Vic managed to do this so successfully that he actually looked as though he was suffering and thinking at the same time, thereby giving a fairly good performance.

I adored Vic and I adored his sense of humour. But many people, particularly women, could not abide

117

him, which was strange since he possessed fantastic good looks – perhaps almost too good! He told me that when he first began in Hollywood he modelled himself on Clark Gable and always tried to conduct his life and career in the same way so that people would be very much in awe of him. Unfortunately, Vic's zest for life and sex were way ahead of Gable's and his sense of humour also got him into trouble. There was the time he described to me when, while under contract to 20th Century Fox, he had a leather jacket made embroidered with the words 'I am the handsomest guy in movies', just to infuriate those who were already jealous of him and very sceptical about his acting ability. Much later in his career he moved out of Hollywood to a ranch and said that the only time he ever went back to Los Angeles was to get a divorce.

In *The Long Haul* Vic played a married lorry-driver whose life became entangled with another woman – and that of course was my role. In real life his capacity for the ladies never ceased to amaze me. Every morning during filming his limousine would arrive at the studio at 8.30 a.m. with a sleeping Vic in the back. There they would leave him until the very last moment, when his various stand-ins and doubles had done all that was possible for him without actually playing the scenes. It was also well-known that Vic never did any of his own fights and that his stand-in, Harold Sanderson, was probably more seen in Mature movies than Vic himself.

I remember on one occasion he decided that he did not want to be made-up for a scene we were doing in a lorry. It was an integral part of the film. There was a long harangue between him and the director, Ken Hughes, with the make-up man hovering nervously about with his sponge covered in Max Factor Pancake Base. Finally Vic relented to the extent that he would only let the make-up man do one side of his face, the side facing the camera. The scene had to be played with him not moving a feature (not even his famous eyebrow acting) for fear the un-made up side would show.

There were many moments on that film, and if they had filmed the 'goings on' between takes it would probably have had much better notices!

Vic had a trailer on set where he kept a constant flow of females lying around waiting for him to have the odd break, or until the real fun began at night. Inside the trailer, he had what he called his 'shit list' marked on the wall. Anyone who transgressed during the day was immediately included on it with a certain number of marks. If they got back into favour their former errors were erased when he was in a good mood, but what his price for coming off the 'shit list' altogether was, I do not know – though if the person were female I can hazard a guess.

As this piece is really supposed to be about lorry drivers and not Victor Mature, I think I had better leave it at that – certainly, there's *no* way I can describe the scene which once took place between Vic and a Spanish maid I employed at the time on my kitchen table! Suffice to say it was witnessed by a rather gruff Colonel and his wife who lived next door and did NOT appreciate it.

## L is for LOVERS

At whatever age a woman takes a lover, it is a wonderful, romantic experience for nothing is more flattering or good for her self-image than to be told and made to feel she is beautiful, desirable and exciting, whether it be across a candlelit dinner table or in the back row of the cinema.

The trouble is that most lovers have a habit of turning into husbands!

# M

## M is for MACHO MEN

Macho is the new word for what we used to call he-men. For some reason all men these days want to be seen as being macho.

I don't want to spoil too many illusions in this book so I'll just say that many Hollywood macho men who make women's hearts flutter are the complete opposite of what they appear to be, particularly the unmarried heart throb who actually wears a pink negligée in bed!

## M is for MAKE-UP

I couldn't decide whether to include this subject in my book but then I caught sight of David Bowie on television and I thought – yes, I must say something about men who wear make-up.

Of course, these days, it is not only restricted to pop stars. Men of all ages are trying out a bit of lip gloss and blusher to see what it does for them, however I don't think I could ever fancy a man who had to disappear to the men's room to touch up his lipstick.

## M is for MALE STRIPPERS

These men are extremely popular in the North where coach-loads of women go on hen-nights to watch some muscle-bound man take his clothes off. The acts are very risqué – and the stripper actually has something hidden in his pants to pull out and titillate the ladies.

I have never seen one myself but I hear there is a male stripper in Gateshead who actually uses live snakes in his act. The mind boggles as to what he does with them!

## M is for MANAGERS

Whenever I read about the husband or lover of a female star and he is described as her 'manager', I'm afraid I regard it somewhat cynically.

This title is usually reserved for those who actually ARE managers, but it's a safe bet that when the man in a woman's life, whether he be tied to her in matrimony or not, passes himself off as her manager, it is merely a courtesy title for someone who is riding on the bandwagon of fame, escorting her to premières, and generally living 'the good life'.

I cannot think offhand of any of these actress/manager combinations making successful, or happy and lasting, relationships. One of the few which springs to mind, of course, was that of Raquel Welch and her 'Svengali'-type husband Patrick Curtis (who was, by the way, the baby in *Gone With The Wind*) but that has nothing to do with what he became in later years. Eventually, during their marriage, his 'managing' became too much for Raquel to handle and she left him.

The only currently successful pair doing the actress/manager routine is Bo Derek and her husband John, so let us hope they prove to be the exceptional ones. After all, Roger Vadim tried hard enough with Brigitte Bardot, Catherine Deneuve and Jane Fonda! All three marriages failed in the end.

However, the aforementioned are simply a few who made the 'manager and actress' syndrome work – as far as their professional lives were concerned anyway!

Susan George split with her boyfriend Derek Webster. He was always referred to as her 'manager' in the days when they went everywhere togethr dripping with gold rings, necklaces, bracelets and all the usual trappings managers often wear.

Hollywood stars Jane Russell and Esther Williams both boasted of husband 'managers' in the good old

121

days, but since their divorces I have not heard of either of those gentlemen managing anyone else.

The late Judy Garland had Sid Luft as her husband and 'manager' for a while in her life, but after their marriage ended he never managed another Judy, not even their daughter Lorna who also attempted to become a singer in her own right.

The list of female stars, including myself, whose love lives have led them to be foolish enough to bestow the title 'manager' on their men is endless. But I suppose the situation will always be the same as long as women allow their hearts to rule their heads.

It is as well that most of them are not as unlucky as one British superstar. When she was attempting to disassociate herself from a lover, whom she had once so fondly spoken of as her 'manager' to the press, he demanded, and got /100,000 in cash for 'services rendered' before he would move his Australian arse from her boudoir.

## M is for BARRY MANILOW
This singer appeals to millions of women to the extent that in Blackpool every so often they have a Barry Manilow weekend which would be fine if he himself came over from the States to meet members of his British fan club. Instead, the organizers wheel out a WAX EFFIGY which the fans queue up to pay homage to. I'm serious!

## M is for CHARLES MANSON
This man should really go under D for Devil because if ever the devil appeared in human form it was in the shape of Charles Manson.

Manson, through his cult following instigated the murder of actress Sharon Tate and is now serving nine life sentences for murder, but he has the audacity to apply for parole!

Twice this mad man has been caught out plotting his escape, but most of the time he has a job as caretaker at the prison chapel where no doubt his religious calling is justified by preaching at the other inmates.

His forehead is still scarred where he used to have a tattoo of a swastika, but now that he has shaven off his beard and all his hair frankly, I think he just looks like any other loony!

## M is for FREDRIC MARCH

The late and great American Oscar-winning actor who gave so many wonderful performances during his life, but whose unfortunate passion for the ladies often got him into trouble, especially with his wife, actress Florence Eldridge. I was sixteen and making a film at a studio in London when he arrived to star in *Christopher Columbus*, heavily guarded by his long-suffering spouse who had craftily got herself a role in the picture so she could really keep an eye on him. Fredric would be seen walking along the studio corridors looking distinguished in his Columbus wig and costume. He had already cast a lecherous eye at me and one day as I was passing his dressing-room an arm shot out and hauled me inside. I found to my dismay that Fredric March was on the other end, and he proceeded to try and make it with me then and there. I struggled free and ran out of the door much to his chagrin, and ever after he became extremely sullen, glowering at me whenever we passed each other.

I was naturally not the only target for his activities. The female hairdresser whose job it was to put on his wig each morning was repeatedly embarrassed by his unsubtle 'groping up her skirt'. One day she could stand it no longer. Throwing down her comb in a rage she exclaimed, 'Mr March, if you don't stop doing that, I am going to put a goddamn rat-trap up there!'

123

*M is for MARRIED MEN*

The world is full of them, and that would be all right if they stayed completely faithful to their wives, but sadly there are very few who do.

Why men bother to get married in the first place, if they still wish to chase women, has always been a mystery, and a subject which has caused great discussion for centuries. Some maintain it is because they have a mother complex and want to recreate her in a wife, some say it is genuinely a need for love, or possibly the nesting syndrome, whilst others insist it might just be an insurance for companionship in old age.

The question was answered most honestly for me by a young television producer one day at rehearsal, as he ricocheted between describing his latest female conquests, and what a drag being married really was, as well as being a restriction on his extra-marital sexual activities.

'Why did you get married at all?' I enquired with genuine female concern.

'It was all because of the great shirt crisis,' he replied glumly.

In one statement I discovered his particular reason for marriage was needing someone to do the washing and ironing. I thanked heaven I was not romatically involved with a married man like him, as some poor unfortunate women might one day be when he gazed into her eyes and told her the tired old chestnut about his wife not really understanding him!

*M is for DEAN MARTIN*

Something about this oh-so-casual, relaxed Italian-American bothers me. For a start, I know his drinking is a big myth which adds a great deal of humour to his image – and goodness knows, when he was teamed with Jerry Lewis, he needed something!

He's always been a handsome, pleasant man, but I

have an uneasy feeling that really he dislikes most people, and although his nightclub act is good, I think his insecurity about his talent shows through which is why he pretends to not give a damn about anyone or anything except Frank Sinatra.

As for his marital status, and the women I know who fancy him as a husband, I have to remind them that he divorced from his second wife Jeanne, a beautiful woman who cared for his four children by a former marriage, and gave him loyal service for many years, in favour of a beauty queen! I rest my case.

*M is for GROUCHO MARX*
One of the all-time great comedians who, along with his equally famous brothers, created comedy in films way back in the thirties which was so ahead of its time and still has present-day audiences falling about – the supreme test of brilliance. Groucho's success has been proved by the fact that he lasted longer than the rest. I met him in Hollywood many years ago when I appeared on a television show he was doing which was a form of 'chat' show with more 'ordinary people appearing on it than celebrities, but all withering under the incredible Groucho wit and wicked cynicism. I had just read a book which had been written about him by his son, describing highly entertaining events in his father's life.

I met him again at a New Year's Eve party, given by the late Jack Benny. This was an annual and very pleasant Hollywood affair to which everyone who was anyone always went. I noticed Groucho with his famous cigar going round to different groups and staying with them until his rather beautiful third wife arrived; then he would immediately move off. He joined my group once or twice and the same thing happened. I did not wonder too much about it as I had met one of my favourite actors, Marlon Brando, who had been extremely complimentary about some film he had seen me in. I was rather lost in the pleasure of his flattery, a situation totally foreign to me in those days as no-one there in Film City had ever seen any of my previous work. As midnight approached I was standing talking to a bunch of people when Groucho appeared again, and I quickly looked to see if his wife had managed to catch up with him this time and hold on, but he was alone. He regaled us with jokes and inevitably we lost track of time. Suddenly we realized it was twelve o'clock and everybody cheered. 'Happy New Year' and 'Auld Lang Syne' were played by the hired orchestra. At this moment Groucho's wife arrived and touched him on the arm. He quickly looked around to see who it was, but on finding that it was his wife, snapped 'A Happy New Year to you Madam, whoever you are,' and ran off.

## M is for MASOCHIST

Aside from a handful of wives who have masochistic husbands and know how to deal with them, prostitutes are the experts on this aspect of masculine behaviour, which is of course, if one analyses it, very 'un-masculine'.

The best story I ever heard was from a prostitute who was paid one hundred pounds a week to visit a man with whom she never spoke. She would enter his flat and put on a slinky evening dress which had been laid out for her in the bedroom. From there she would proceed to the bathroom where a full bath of water awaited her and, having plunged in, would then rise like a rather soapy version of Venus from the sea, with the driss clinging tightly to her body. At this moment our hero, the masochist, ran in, screamed in horror (or maybe it was sexual frenzy) and ran out again. What strange creatures men can be!

There was also a Hollywood male star who could

only get his sexual thrills by being handcuffed to the bed . . . but that's another story!

## M is for PAUL McCARTNEY

The richest man in British showbusiness but no-one would ever know it! His wife Linda saves scraps, uses up leftovers and scrimps as though she's down to her last fiver.

Perhaps if he did go on a spending spree both of them would look happier in newspaper photographs.

## M is for JOHN McENROE

This brilliant champion might be advised to have his jaws wired up as drastic slimmers do before entering the court, thus giving those long-suffering umpires a rest as well as the opportunity to concentrate on his tennis instead of his tongue!

## M is for MICK McGAHEY

I am totally ignorant of politics, but I do not like Communists, and of all the Reds under the beds in Britain, the one I like least is this one.

Having watched him snarling on television – the only place I am ever likely to have to witness his ramblings – I find myself sympathising with Mrs McGahey, and wondering how she could ever have fallen for, let alone married, such a nasty man.

I also remember an occasion when he became so enraged in some political argument that the collar of his shirt shot up on one side like a pointed arrow. I'll bet he blamed her lack of prowess as a launderess when he got home and watched the re-run on video.

## M is for MILITARY MEN

My father was a Captain in the first world war but thankfully, unlike some, refused to carry his title on into civilian life as many egotistical men do. Hence the awe we are supposed to feel when introduced to Major this, Colonel that, or even Wing Commander Kite!

Despite his readiness to leave the army behind him, however, the military descipline rubbed off in many ways. He used to point his forefinger at my mother and myself, rather like a gun, when ordering us to do something, and directed routine household chores as if shouting at an entire regiment of soldiers.

Our plight was not as bad as that of a schoolfriend I had whose father had also occupied the rank of Captain, and carried both the title and position into their family existence with such fervour that the whole house was run like an army barracks, even to only a certain number of inches of water being allowed per bath.

Uniforms do strange things to men, and for the life of me I cannot imagine women strutting around in the same manner, although I suppose there are always a few bossy ones at school, and other places, who disprove the theory. I often wonder though if there are ANY hen-pecked Sergeant Majors at home? I am sure there are not!

*M is for MILKMEN*
I once made a film entitled *The Amorous Milkman* and the actor who played the title role got up to all kinds of naughty pranks.

Whether milkmen really are over-sexed, stopping to dally with hard-working husband's bored wives instead of delivering the milk as they should be doing, I do not know. It could be they are a much maligned breed! Certainly my own neither turns me on nor is even on time with the morning order. Neither does he come in for a cuppa or anything else! But they do say there is no smoke without fire and all those sexy stories about milkmen must have originated somehow!

128

*M is for MILLIONAIRES*

This is the ultimate dream male for any woman to find, but they are very few and far between, as anyone who is searching will verify. Besides, by the time a girl starts looking, and a man has made his millions, he will almost certainly have a wife! The best she can hope for then is to become his mistress.

To be a successful mistress, which also comes under the letter M, is something that takes an enormous amount of intelligence to accomplish, but is always defeated by old age. As the song goes, 'It's then that those louses go back to their spouses! So diamonds truly are a girl's best friend.'

Film star Zsa Zsa Gabor, herself no slouch at finding a millionaire or two in her time, once came completely unstuck, despite her shrewdness, when she met what she thought was a Texan oil magnate worth vast fortunes. What neither of them knew as they solemnly took their marriage vows was that he was broke, and she did NOT command twenty thousand dollars every time she opened a supermarket, which is what he fervently believed. The awful crunch came when he swept her off to his little apartment in Dallas, and expected her to wash his socks – which is what we all know any man will do, millionaire or not.

*M is for ROBERT MORLEY*

One of my favourite gentlemen – we have a great deal in common when it comes to loving food.

I think he often pretends to eat more than he really does because it makes a good story. I have seen him on American television explaining in a very amusing manner the delights of English treacle puddings! To my amazement, for all his exremely aristocratic lifestyle he is a red hot Socialist, whereas Ken Dodd, the working man's favourite, is a staunch Tory. Oh well!

You just never can tell with men, especially actors and comedians!

## M is for MOSES
All women know how difficult most husbands can be at the best of times . . . imagine what it must have been like being married to the one who brought down the commandments for EVERYONE to obey?

## M is for OSWALD MOSLEY
Sir Oswald saw me on television and wrote an article for the *Sunday Times* in which he said I was the best thing to happen to this country in years. In fact he put me on a par with the only other woman who he said was of any importance at all, namely Margaret Thatcher.

I now have the distinction of being accused by the late Archbishop of Canterbury of being a wayward hussy and complimented by a politician whose briliant career was halted only by his Fascist leanings.

## M is for MUSCLEMEN
I once had an affair with a muscleman and nearly died of boredom! The only thing he was interested in was lifting his wretched dumb-bells and improving his physique.

I suppose every woman at some time in their lives falls for a muscleman. Jayne Mansfield had Micky Hargitay who it is rumoured she stole from Mae West. Mae, crafty old bird that she was, had spotted Micky much earlier and put him in her show. She was very peeved when Jayne ran away with him.

Whether he had a great physique to go with his fabulous set of muscles I don't really know, for when I met him a couple of times in Hollywood with Jayne in the true style of most musclemen he remained as dumb as the bells he lifted.

# N

## N is for NAMBY-PAMBY

We all know a namby-pamby – a grown man who acts like a child when something goes wrong. I didn't realize until the other day that there was such a person as Namby Pamby and he WAS a man.

Dear old Ambrose Philips who lived about 300 years ago, wrote poems for children and got the name of Namby. Pamby was added on, for the children I suppose, because it sounded better. Ambrose was no Namby-Pamby but there are a good many around today.

## N is for NAMES

'What's in a name?' wrote William Shakespeare, 'A rose by any other name would smell as sweet.'

Perhaps so – but we all have the right to change our names if we're stuck with a bad one from the start.

Thankfully, I changed my surname from 'Fluck', to my grandmother's maiden name, 'Dors', otherwise 'Diana Fluck' may have flickered dangerously up there in neon lights!

Actors are slightly different from ordinary men, in so much as they have to put on various masks throughout their lives on stage in order to portray all kinds of roles, therefore it is hardly surprising that many change their names to conform with the image they wish to present to the world.

'When a man puts on make-up,' said one jaded Hollywood director with whom I once worked, 'he ceases to become a real man.'

Maybe that is true to an extent, but I do not think that the likes of Clint Eastwood or Robert Redford are in any way feminine.

However, a name *is* important to an actor or singer, as in the case of the singer Tom Jones, who changed his surname from Woodward at a time when there was an extremely provocative film going the rounds as he began his career, entitled *Tom Jones* and starring Albert Finney (an actor who stuck to his guns and steadfastly refused to alter his name by the way).

To prove my point further I have to say that women would not have thrilled to the sound of Maurice Micklewhite as they did to Michael Caine, or succumbed to the charms of Archibald Leach who became suave Cary Grant.

Bernie Schwartz quickly transformed himself into Tony Curtis and was followed by an entire group of Hollywood hopefuls who changed their somewhat ordinary monikers to names like Rock Hudson, Rip Torn, Beau Gentry and Tab Hunter to mention just a few.

And with all due respect to the late John Wayne, he could hardly have strutted through the dust in the macho manner we all came to love as 'Marion Mitchell', his original name.

*N is for NANNY LOVER*

Most men born to families wealthy enough to employ a nanny for them in childhood seem to revere such women with more respect and love than they do their mothers.

It is well known that Winston Churchill idolized his nanny 'Womany' throughout his entire life, visiting her and confiding in her far more than his famous and beautiful mother Jenny.

When great statesmen like this behave like small boys where nannies are concerned, it is not difficult to understand the likes of film actor Stewart Granger, I suppose, who confided one evening at a Hollywood dinner party to anyone interested enough to listen that the only sort of woman who really turned him on sexually must look and behave like a big, stout Nanny.

It is easy to see the attraction for his first wife actress Elspet March who, with all due respect, reached quite large proportions as she grew older, but one wonders where his head was when he married Jean Simmons way back in 1950! Not to mention a young Belgian beauty queen named Caroline after that.

Perhaps the reason all three marriages ended in divorce was because none of them were strong enough to lift him out of the bath and pat him dry cosily in a towel.


## N is for NAPOLEON

This little dictator was no doubt a brilliant soldier, but from the way he treated Josephine he was quite obviously one of the early French male chauvinists!

If only she had turned the tables on him, thus striking a blow for women. Today we could all quote the now famous sentence as, 'Not tonight "short-arse" not tonight'!


## N is for NARCISSUS

This attractive boy saw his reflection in a pool and, thinking he was looking at a beautiful nymph, dived in . . . and drowned. How silly can you get? One of the first lessons everyone learns in life is to look before you leap.

Still it is this young man we have to thank for the lovely springtime flower. According to the same legend the nymphs came for his body but found only a flower which they called Narcissus.

*N is for NERO*
One of the most famous of the Roman Emperors whose fiddling whilst Rome burned has gone down as one of the maddest acts in history.

Compared with the exploits of some of the others dealt with in this book under E for Emperors I suppose his behaviour was fairly mild, although I cannot imagine a woman doing it, can you?

*N is for PAUL NEWMAN*
This brilliant actor has been nominated for an Oscar so many times but has never landed one. It must be particularly galling when his wife Joanne Woodward has actually received one herself.

Paul's latest chance was for his superb performance in the film *Verdict*, but he was up against Ben Kingsley who starred in Richard Attenborough's celebrated epic, *Ghandi*.

Ben won, and yet again Paul Newman had to be a good loser. In fact being a good loser must come easier to him now for he says he makes a point of turning up to the Oscar ceremony so that no-one can accuse him of going off in a huff.

Actually it says much for this blue-eyed charmer's sense of humour that after being beaten by Britain's Ben Kingsley he was seen wearing a T-shirt that had a picture of Ben as Ghandi on, with Paul Newman trying to strangle him!

He is a gorgeous hunk of masculinity that neither man nor woman could criticize, but he's also far from perfect if the hints his wife drops are anything to go by. However they have been married now for twenty-five years, and in a rare interview Paul revealed why the relationship has lasted so long. He said, 'We live in a throw-away society. We throw away bottles and cans and children and careers and wives and marriages.

'But Joanne and I work at ours. We fix the toaster if it breads and we fix our marriage when it is strained.'

There are a lot of men out there who would do well to try and follow that advice.

*N is for ROBERT NEWTON*

The most controversial and colourful character England has uver produced, and a brilliant actor in to the bargain.

The stories about his professional and private life are unending, and when a group of people who knew him sit down for an evening, they can usually exchange so many tales about him there is no room for other conversation. His drinking was, I suppose, the thing that triggered off most of his escapades, such as the occasion when he staggered into Dame Anna Neagle's dressing room exposing himself in front of a group of ladies as she was serving them tea, or the night in Rome when he threw a party in a nightclub and brought champagne all round, knowing full well he could not pay the bill. Long before the management could settle the matter, he pretended his wallet had been stolen and sneaked away to the airport where he was catching a plane to England.

Newton left this country some years before his death under a terrible cloud and never returned. He had nearly come to the end of a film entitled *Trilby and Svengali* when his marriage problems got the better of him, so he grabbed his baby son in a carry cot and left these shores vowing not to return. He must have known he was committing professional suicide, for no film company would ever employ or insure him again. As it was the entire film had to be recast and shot at unbelieveable expense. Right or wrong, I admired the man, for at least he had the courage of his convictions. Many actors TALK about doing things, but that is as far as they get.

Probably the funniest story about Newton happened many years before he had attained stardom. He was touring as the Duke of Buckingham in a Shakespearian play with another fine actor and drinker, the late Wilfred Lawson. Naturally the pair got on very well, and did a great deal of heavy drinking together, but it never affected their performances. One day, however, the worst happened. Both drunk as monkeys, they staggered along a street and upon seeing a fishmongers' shop with all the cods heads laid out on the slab, Wilfred was reminded that they had a matinee that very afternoon. 'My God, Robert. We've got a matinee!' he exclaimed, and pulled Newton off as fast as he could.

On arrival at the theatre they rushed headlong into their dressing rooms and proceeded to try to climb into their costumes. Wilfred was in such a state he put his tights on the wrong way, thereby making his codpiece look like a diseased hip but, undaunted, he hit the stage just in time for his cue. Owing to his inebriated state he began reeling off the lines in such a way that they made no sense whatsoever, and it was quite apparent that he was tipsy!

Unable to stand the performance he was giving any longer, someone from the gallery shouted out, 'You're pissed'.

Wilfred stopped dead in his tracks, looked up into the darkness and remembering that his friend Newton had not yet made his entrance snarled, 'You think I'm pissed? . . . Just wait until you see the Duke of Buckingham'!

## N is for NEWSREADERS

Have you noticed – it is always women newsreaders who go on to make a success of their lives – and it can't all be down to good looks.

Selina Scott, Angela Rippon, Anna Ford, have all

amassed fortunes thanks to the start they got reading television news bulletins. But can you think of a famous man who *used* to read the news aside form poor old Reggie Bosanquet? And one could hardly call his career successful nowadays.

## N is for DAVID NIVEN
What epitaph could anyone write, that has not already been done before, about this debonair actor, author and witty raconteur.

It was one of the greatest regrets of my life never to have met the man behind the public image, but I am sure that now he has left us there is much laughter in Paradise, whilst we mere mortals are down here trying to get along without him.

## N is for Noah
He must have been the first male chauvinist, for his wife's actual name is never referred to in the Bible.

## N is for RUDOLPH NUREYEV
Like everyone else, I am a great admirer of this fabulous ballet dancer, but unfortunately the occasion I met him was not as artistically choreographed as his theatre productions.

Nureyev was brought to my house one Sunday afternoon quite unexpectedly and had I known of his impending arrival I would have made arrangements accordingly, for it was not every day I had an international star of such magnitude gate-crashing my home on the off-chance of a cup of tea.

From the start things went wrong. His entrance, swathed in white leather from head to foot and looking rather like Marlene Dietrich, was obviously intended to be somewhat spectacular and get us all going, but unluckily for him the whole thing was marred by bad timing. An old flame of mine with whom I have stayed friends all these years, namely 'Dandy' Kim Waterfield, chose quite coincidentally to make a descent into the garden in his gleaming new blue and white helicopter, which was a very difficult arrival for anyone to compete against. As everyone milled around Kim and his aircraft, admiring it, asking what it was like to fly around in, and pop down to friends' houses miles away for a drink, Nureyev quietly slunk into the drawing-room, white leather and all, and hunched in an armchair looking extremely sullen.

Surprisingly enough, no-one really took very much notice of him. Indeed the only ones who showed him any attention at all were my two boxer dogs, who leapt all around him with their usual high spirits, looking somewhat like canine Nureyevs themselves!

Relations between East and West were not entirely improved when a boyfriend of mine who happened to be in residence playing host that day, asked him what he would like to drink, and received the rather haughty reply, 'I only drink Russian Vodka.' My boyfriend, taken slightly aback by this statement on a Sunday afternoon in the country, and a trifle worried as he knew there was none, jokingly replied, 'I'm sorry we don't have any of that, but if you fancy it there's a bottle of Tizer in the fridge.'

An hour or so rolled by and still only the dogs and Nureyev were making contact. Actually thinking back to some of the people there at the time, he was probably happier to remain in the company of canines than humans, for not another word passed his lips after the Tizer affair.

During the afternoon, however, I saw Nureyev slip through the French windows when no-one was looking, and presumed he was merely going to accompany his doggy friends on a stroll around the garden. Some minutes later I perceived the dogs joyfully 'cocking their legs' in the rhododendron bushes, but Nureyev decided to go one better! Having slyly surveyed the offending aircraft which had stolen his thunder, he got his revenge by relieving himself against the tail!

I can assure my reader it was not the sort of performance for which he usually received great acclaim from a Covent Garden audience, and it would certainly not have been artistically appreciated by Kim either, who at that moment was blissfully unaware his machine was being defiled.

Finally it was time to go, but his exit was eclipsed by the sudden and once again unwitting decision on Kim's part to leave at the same time. As Nureyev crept out of the door, the rest of the party did not even see him go, for they were all too busy waving goodbye in the heavy downdraft of the helicopter.

If all this seems like a rather rude reception for so talented a person, then it is with sincerity I extend my belated apologies to Rudolph Nureyev and promise that next time he ever graces my home, I will be sure to have more than a bottle of Tizer put aside for him.

## N is for NYMPHOMANIAC

Make no mistake. The problem of being a nymphomaniac is not reserved to the female sex. The male nymphomaniac is the nervous energy type who often cannot sit still for one minute because he is usually dashing around all over the place trying to prove his virility and expertise in bed.

This man thinks he is the world's best lover. A bit like the one who goes into a restaurant full of gorgeous things to eat. He is unable to choose so he orders some of everything, but once he has had a taste he in no longer interested any more.

I have read books on the subject of male nymphomania and it is far worse than the female kind, probably because men do not recognize it in themselves, preferring to think they are Casanovas, or at the very least 'Jack the lads'!

I once knew a man suffering from this who even though married to one of Hollywood's most beautiful women and quite a dish himself where looks were concerned, behaved appallingly with each and every woman he could get his hands on, and I mean that literally.

Misguidedly I arranged for him to escort a young starlet to a film première one evening, because she needed an escort, and his wife was away working as usual to support him and their children.

Before the chauffeur-driven limousine had left the driveway of my house where the two had just been formally introduced, he was forcing his hands up the poor girl's dress, so heaven knows what else he attempted in the darkness of the cinema!

Suffice it to say she telephoned me the next morning complaining about my choice of companion for her and of course, she was absolutely justified. My anger and surprise at his behaviour, for I had never heard of a male nymphomaniac before (men had always been so eager to describe female ones to me) was realized much later when, in desperation, having tried to have sex with as many women as his insatiable appetite required over the years, he finally raped his own wife in front of their two daughters.

Needless to say, the marriage ended in bitter divorce, and no doubt he became, as most nymphomaniacs do, a lonely, pathetic human being, with only sordid memories for comfort.

# O

*O is for OLD MEN*
'Old men promise what young men deliver'!

*O is for OLIVER*
I have followed Oliver Reed's career and frantic attempts to be a hell-raiser, drinker and womanizer with great amusement.

He is attractive, of course. But I do not like the way he knocks his fellow actors in print. On one occasion he even turned on poor Raquel Welch, after a film they had made together, saying she was not as sexy as him.

In her defence alone I must state that Oliver Reed has not always been the strong, masculine hunk he is seen to be on screen.

Way back in 1955 when I was starring in a comedy film called *Value for Money*, who should come mincing on with one line as a 'fairy' chorus boy but our Oliver!

I realize that all actors have to start somewhere, and I often look back and shudder at many of my old films on television, but at least I have never appeared as a butch lesbian!

*O is for SIR LAURENCE OLIVIER*
I consider this noble knight to be the only actor in England to really warrant a title. He is now, of course, Lord Olivier, but when I first met him he was still a Sir.

My heart beat excitedly when I was told that he was in the audience at a theatre where I was enjoying a fantastic success in a revue back in 1952. He had come to 'look me over', as they say, for a film he was about to make entitled *The Beggar's Opera*, but it never came to fruition for I had so many offers on the strength of my success that for the first time in my career I did not know which one to accept, and I was just twenty years old.

The next time we met was at the première of my best film, *Yield to the Night*. He was there alone and after the performance he came up to me and said, 'Bravo'. One word from an actor like Olivier is worth a thousand more from others.

The years went by and my career went steadily down and down, until by the middle sixties I was forced to leave my children in Hollywood where we had all been living, and come home to England in order to make money by trading on a screen name that had once been big. I started doing cabaret in working men's clubs all over the country, cracking jokes about my former sexy image, and putting up with all the shouting, leering and in some cases bottle throwing that went on whilst I was on stage.

On one occasion I was due to appear in Newcastle at a club, and as it was Good Friday the manager had been refused a licence to open, so I was left with an evening to spare. The stately drama theatre was boasting a production which starred Michael Redgrave and Joan Plowright, Lady Olivier, as she was by then. Sir Cedric Hardwicke, a marvellous actor of many Hollywood films, had a son named Edward, and he invited me to see the play that evening.

Afterwards he insisted we go back stage to congratulate Joan on her performance. I did not know her, but he assured me she knew we were going to be in the audience and wanted to meet me. Sure enough she greeted me with great warmth, and after an amusing half hour in the dressing room, invited us both back to the hotel where she and Sir Laurence were staying. I declined at once, muttering something about 'his not wanting to see me at that time of night', but she refused to listen and ushered us into her waiting car and back to the hotel for supper.

Sir Laurence greeted me with the same warmth his wife had shown, and as we talked my eye caught sight of a salad supper for two laid on the table in the corner. 'Heavens,' I thought, 'they were going to dine together alone, and now I'm here.' Knowing English hotels I also realized that after a certain time there was no chance of an added order or two being sent up.

I chattered on and eventually Joan said, 'Come on, Diana, sit here with me and let's eat, you must be starving. 'But what about you?' I asked Sir Laurence. 'Oh never mind,' he answered gallantly, 'I had something earlier on, just tuck in.' I knew he was merely being courteous and Edward Hardwicke who probably felt as embarrassed as I, hastily said he had eaten too, which I knew was untrue for he had been with me all evening.

Desperately I tried not to steal Sir Laurence's supper and continued to argue, but he finally pushed me into his chair at the table and made me eat.

As the night wore on, and I began to relax, we became great friends, sitting there until four in the morning telling stories and jokes which had us all crying with laughter. I also found his language as salty as mine which came as a surprise, but a nice one, for I remember thinking that here was probably the greatest and most respected actor in the world – and he was as natural and human as it was possible for anyone to be!

Long, long after that night in Newcastle, which hardly sounds as glamorous as say 'that night in Monte Carlo', I was making a film in Pinewood and lunching in the studio restaurant heavily disguised with a red wig. Suddenly, there was a flurry near my table and

143

up came Lord Olivier, as he was by then, arms outstretched, uttering cries of welcome.

I do not know how he knew it was me under all that make-up, for he was the only one in that restaurant that did, but the incident touched me. It also impressed everybody else there too, for the film's publicity man came up to me later that afternoon and informed me the whole studio was buzzing with the news that Lord Olivier had actually seen fit to come to my table. Such is show business!

*O is for OMAR*

When the sultry, dark-eyed, sexy Mr Sharif first rode on to the screen in *Lawrence of Arabia* most women, including me, were breathless with excitement, panting to be carried off by him into the desert.

No-one could understand why the ex-Mrs Sharif had allowed him to get away in real life, but as time went on it became increasingly obvious. She probably could not wait to see the back of him, for that is precisely what she had been looking at all through their married life . . . his back!

It appears the only two things that really get him steamed up are bridge and backgammon.

Hardly any woman's idea of a thrilling Egyptian knight!

*O is for 007*

Although he is no angel where women are concerned, I like Sean Connery because he is honest and down to earth.

Dismissing George Lazenby who blew his big chance (the part most actors would give their teeth to play), the subject of James Bond brings me to Roger Moore.

I have known this particular 007 for nearly thirty years. We met when he was playing the King in pantomime with his second wife singer Dorothy

Squires, and if you want to know what he is really like, ask Dot!

It is not for me to criticize him for dumping her in favour of another, after she first took him to Hollywood and helped him while he waited for his career to take off. But I can state that an enormous change has come over Roger since he finally got the stardom he so desperately sought.

However, according to comedienne Hylda Baker, herself a close friend of the couple during the early years they were together and Dorothy Squires was the star of the family, I am wrong about this.

Lunching with Hylda one day at Pinewood studios I watched, fascinated, as Roger made what can only be described as a 'superstar' entrance into the restaurant.

'How he has altered,' I said sadly. 'Once upon a time he was fun to be with, and not at all conceited.'

'Rubbish,' said Hylda shrewdly. 'If you think about it, deep down he was always a shit. It just took success to bring it out!'

*O is for ORIENTALS*
Surveys show that women in general do not go for oriental men, whereas most men, if given the chance, would adore a subservient Oriental woman, pandering to them, preferably on their knees, Geisha style. Frankly, I'd run a mile if I found a Japanese man in my bedroom – perhaps I've seen too many war films!

145

# P

*P is for IAN PAISLEY*
How this man dares to wear a clerical collar, and call
himself a servant of God, is beyond me.

The thing I loathe most in life is hypocrisy and if
anyone personifies this it is the reverend(?) himself.
He has to be the worst thing that ever happened to
religion but Heaven forbid anyone assassinates him
and makes him a martyr.

*P is for MICHAEL PARKINSON*
He has said himself that he is a male chauvinist pig. I
can elaborate no further!

*P is for NICHOLAS PARSONS*
Honestly, straight up, I have never yet met a man or
woman, who does not seem to find this man anything
but a pompous, crashing bore.

Obviously from the smile on his school-masterly
face, and probably from the size of his bank account
(for he has been in show-business THAT long), one
way and another Nicholas is delighted with himself
and considers he has oodles of talent.

I dare anyone to stare him right in the eyeball and
tell him he hasn't!

*P is for PERFECT MAN*
P is for perfect man . . . sadly I'm afraid there is no
such animal!

## P is for PISCES

Piscean men are all right, and quite good fun if you catch them in the right mood. The thing that really bothers me are those two fish swimming in opposiste directions!

## P is for PLUMBERS

Plumbers are not always stout, elderly men who arrive at your house armed with a sink plunger! If your pipes are blocked up, a young plumber can also soon sort them out . . . but be sure your husband is at home when he comes!

The last one to visit me in an emergency had obviously been told he looked like England's answer to Robert Redford, and his jeans fitted so tightly there was hardly room for his tool kit!

## P is for POLICEMEN

I know one has to fight fire with fire and that policemen are a very important part of our society. Having said that, I can only say that any man who has to swear on oath that he will 'turn his own parents in' if necessary can't be ALL bad!

## P is for POLITICIANS

Since the downfall of the government back in the 1960s when Harold Macmillan took a dive over the Christine Keeler affair and, more recently, the Jeremy Thorpe scandal, many politicians have been subject to all sorts of conjecture about their lives, in and out of politics.

Today, rumours run rife regarding ex-Prime Ministers' and MP's private perversions, but that is their business as far as I am concerned. What annoys me, where politicians are concerned, is the fact that professionally they will NEVER give anyone a straight answer! Indeed, all of them are masters of the art of confusing the public and ducking important questions.

However, it is men we are discussing in this book and I can imagine how awful life is for the wives of these political males, particularly when they have lost an election (which more often than not the wives have helped them campaign for) or arrived home late at night after a bad argument in the House of Commons.

Living at number 10 with the now Lady Falkender, then Harold Wilson's secretary and guru, must have been pure hell for Mary Wilson at times, as 'Marcia' literally ran the roost if we are to believe what we read in the press.

The late Lloyd George was such a great womanizer (as his long-suffering wife would testify if she were still around) that his extra-marital affairs were actually made into a successful television series.

But the final word on the subject of politicians as husbands and lovers, come from an MP himself, Nicholas Fairbairn, dubbed 'Dandy Nick' at Westminster, because of his flashy style of dress, a far cry from Michael Foot, and regarded as the Tory's own sex symbol!

Having dissolved his first marriage and lived through one suicide attempt by a mistress, besides admitting in a newspaper article on 'Love, Power and Politics' to having lusted after ladies since he was eight, Mr Fairbairn states quite openly that in his opinion 'A sexy mistress, is better than a boring wife', as recently, deposed minister Cecil Parkinson would probably agree.

## P is for PONTIUS PILATE

Whilst holding no brief for this man, I have to say that in one sense I feel a little sorry for him.

If we are to believe it was all prophesied and written before their time then he, like Judas, had no option but to do what he did! However, if he had only listened to his wife when she told him of the dream she experienced, perhaps things might have been different?

## P is for POOR MEN
Film starlet and raver extraordinaire, Linda Christian, who discovered Errol Flynn and was once married to Tyrone Power, once said, 'It is just as easy to love a rich man as a poor man.'

## P is for POP SINGERS
I cannot think that being married to a pop-singer is all 'beer and skittles' as the saying goes.

Most girls, particularly 'groupies' who travel around with the bands, have a fascination for these young musicians whilst in their teens, but luckily very few actually become involved with them seriously in something like marriage, and I choose my words carefully!

If a girl is unfortunate enough to find herself with a pop-singer for a husband, then she has to be prepared to hardly ever see him whilst he is 'out on the road'. She also has to endure women throwing themselves at him everywhere he goes . . . as the long suffering Mrs Tom Jones will testify!

Even coping successfully with this state of affairs does not always bring lasting happiness either and many wives feel lost and left out of things as the years go by.

Each of the first marriages of the Beatles ended in divorce, as did Mick Jagger's and dozens of others too numerous to mention here.

Perhaps one of the saddest was that of Paul Jones, late of the Manfred Mann group, who subsequently became a film actor.

After many years together, plus two children, he and his wife separated; but instead of reaping whatever benefits there are of being wed to a pop star like Paul, his now ex-wife Sheila claims she is poverty-stricken and destitute, to the extent she is trying to make ends meet by bringing out a book she has penned all about 'broken marriages'!

May I suggest the title *Heartbreak Hotel?*

## P is for POSTMEN

*The Postman Always Rings Twice* was the name of a film which oddly has also been *made* twice.

Though neither offering was really anything to do with the world of postmen, it is interesting that the title conjures up a somewhat exciting image of them. Certainly the male stars of both movies, whilst not actually portraying postmen are, and were, highly over-sexed men, whose private lives rated possibly steamier headlines than the film itself.

The late John Garfield died in bed with a woman, some say whilst actually in the act of making love. Even though he was a sex-symbol of his day and lusted after by thousands of women, Garfield's passions in his last years could only be aroused by coloured whores.

Jack Nicholson was the second 'Postman' and still lays claim to being Hollywood's naughty boy! Having experimented with all kinds of drugs, and for that matter all kinds of women after his divorce, Nicholson's most unusual act was to put cocaine on various parts of his body during sex. Whether he still employs this form of stimulation I don't know.

All in all, neither actor has the slightest connection with ordinary postmen going about their daily deliveries but I thought their various exploits would make amusing reading. Speaking for myself however, on the subject of what it must be like to be married to a postman, I have to say that these ladies have my highest esteem . . . let's face it, how would YOU like a husband who gets out of bed each morning around four-thirty, in order to go off and ring some other woman's doorbell!

*P is for PRINCES*
'Some day my prince will come', goes the song. In Princess Diana's case it happened, but to most women it never does. However, film actresses Dawn Adams and Jackie Lane might have different versions of just how rotten catching a prince and marrying him really can be. Certainly their experiences would not fit the fantasy we all have about living happily after!

# Q

*Q is for QUALITY*
I suppose the old adage about 'quality, not quantity' is one of the most important things for women to remember, where men are concerned!

*Q is for the QUEEN*
Deviating from this book about men for a moment, I think the Queen is a wonderful woman and I am privileged to have actually been presented to her. She is warm and kind and has a knack of putting nervous people at their ease.

However her life is not all easy and she often has a rough time. Visiting Australia some time ago (Lord Snowdon was still married to Princess Margaret), Her Majesty had experienced a pretty difficult tour, for Australians are not exactly the most sophisticated race and many of the press photographers had had great difficulty getting the pictures they wanted to send round the world.

'I know how hard it has been for you all,' said the Queen graciously in her farewell speech 'because my brother-in-law is a photographer.'

In one of those awful silent pauses, a big Aussie voice piped up from the back, 'Oh yeah, and my brother-in-law is a queen.'

*Q is for QUEENS*
A marvellous story about Queens is credited to the Queen Mother. Apparently having come downstairs to the massive kitchen of her home one morning to find

two members of her staff who were obviously gay having a temperamental dispute and screaming at each other as only gays can.

'It seems I'm not the only Queen in this house,' she announced majestically.

## Q is for QUIPS
The brilliant actor Sir Alec Guiness once said, 'I don't know who I am. Quite possibly I do not exist at all'!

How confusing for his wife!

## Q is for QUOTES
Quotes are fascinating to pick up, and who better to make a few scintillating ones on the subject of men, than the late, great Mae West, who said, amongst other things: 'It's not the men in my life, it's the life in my men!'

'Thanks I enjoyed every inch of it!'

'Every man I meet wants to protect me – can't figure out from whom?'

'It takes two to make trouble for one!'

'A man has more character in his face at 30 than 20 – he's suffered longer!'

'Sex is an emotion. Love conquers all things except poverty and toothache!'

Obviously I cannot leave the last word to Mae, but must include one of my own which is: 'Men are like safety pins. Either they pin you down or leave you undone'!

# R

*R is for RAPISTS*
All right, all right, I know there are many older married women who are reputed to have led young boys astray, but I doubt if any man would be frightened to walk home alone for fear of being raped by a woman.

*R is for RONALD REAGAN*
I know nothing about American politics, but I am sure that this Hollywood actor turned politician means well, and has certainly done his best whilst acting again, this time as President of the United States!

Obviously Reagan's success basically lies in the fact that as an ex-actor he knows exactly how to deliver a speech with all the emotion, flair, and timing necessary to send his audience wild with excitement whatever the subject may be.

Apparently he did not send his first wife Jane Wyman, herself an Oscar winner, wild about anything in their personal life together (which is what really matters in a relationship between a man and a woman) and that is what we are discussing throughout this book. After tolerating what she described as a boring marriage for as many years as she could and listening, as wives have to do, to the same old stories, in Ronnie's case political ones, she finally snapped one morning at breakfast and poured a bowl of oatmeal over his head!

I met Reagan once at a Hollywood party given by the late Jack Benny and he told me, along with several others, one of the dirtiest stories I have ever heard. Perhaps he forgot to tell it to Jane! Certainly if he had tried to amuse her more she might be the First Lady of America today instead of Nancy, and anti-Reagan campaigners would not have printed the badges which they distributed throughout the land claiming 'JANE WYMAN WAS RIGHT!'

## R is for BURT REYNOLDS
The current heart-throb who sends shivers up and down women's spines is handsome and sexy it's true, but his marital track record with British actress Judy Carne left much to be desired. After he posed full-frontal nude in a magazine after their divorce, Judy did point out that Burt only needed *one* hand to cover the part most women wanted to see.

## R is for RICHARD III
Richard the hunchback was a much-maligned king and whether he deserved it we shall never know. He is blamed for the murder of the little Princes in the Tower and indeed may well have been guilty of the terrible crime against his two innocent nephews.

In his day he was reputed to be the handsomest man in England but, as the saying goes, it is the evil a man does that lives after him.

Richard may not have done any evil, but his reputation certainly lives on these hundreds of years later.

## R is for ROMANS
Life must have been fantastic in those far-off Roman days of banquets, orgies and battles, but if women are looking for something similar today they will be sadly disappointed. Frankly, the only Roman men around now are puny little shadows of their glorious ancestors.

## R is for ROMANTICISTS

Sadly, there are so very few of these left in the world today that most married women, instead of being pleased when their husband brings them home flowers or a present, become immediately suspicious.

Poets are true romantics, and the great playright Christopher Marlowe once said that, 'Only a poet may dine with lords, and sup with cut-throats.' Somehow I cannot picture Robert Browning doing the latter at any time!

## R is for ROUMANIANS

Roumanian men are, by and large, a romantic lot, not at all like their near Russian counterparts, interested or good at the art of fighting and soldiering.

Roumanian film director Jean Negulesco one time-gigolo in Paris, artist extraordinaire in the world of painting, and the man responsible for making such artistic films as *Three Coins In THe Fountain* and *How To Marry A Millionaire*, was discussing the 1982 Falklands war with me one day, as we basked in the sunshine at his Spanish holiday home.

Like most men who are not English and cannot understand our temperament or patriotism, Jean disapproved entirely of the whole thing, arguing heatedly that it was all a complete waste of life and time.

In vain I attempted to put forward the British point of view, maintaining that the Argentinians had no right to behave as they had, but Jean would not give in,

'The Falklands war was ridiculous,' he declared, 'It was exactly like two bald headed old men fighting over a comb!'

## R is for RUSSIANS

I have not met many Russian men so I am not qualified to speak about their capabilities as lovers or husbands, though I suspect Christina Onassis may now have some doubtful tales to tell in that department, having failed in her attempt to become a Moscow housewife.

All I can say is that any race of men who swill vodka in copious quantities and perform the sort of dance we have all observed Cossacks doing, which resembles something close to Olympic athletes having their braces caught up in their bootlaces, cannot be much use to any woman when they finally fall into bed.

# S

## S is for SAGITTARIUS

Sagittarian men are lovely people who adore life and exult in large gatherings or company, but woe betide a girl if she gets stuck with one for a husband!

Whilst he may thrill and amuse her during courtship, when she finally tries to pin him down in wedlock he will spend most of his time trying to get out of the house and escape.

These men hate to be confined, and their heads are constantly in the clouds. They aim their arrows at the stars which is all great fun if you happen to meet one at a party, but the problem maritally is that they neither see nor care about the poor unfortunate partner whose own zodiac sign tendencies are being crushed beneath their feet.

## S is for SALESMEN

Like the much-maligned milkmen, this particular breed also come under a great deal of fire regarding their activities during working hours. Perhaps this is because there do appear to be a great many bored, frustrated lady housewives (due of course to a lack of enthusiasm from their husbands). Really, it is once again the fault of the men if their wives' eyes start rolling in the direction of a smooth-talking fellow standing at the front door, eager to please.

I once heard a strange tale from the mother of one of these salesmen! The lady herself worked for me as a domestic help, and expressed her concern at the amount of women with whom her son seemed to have physical contact during the course of his work. It was not that she minded for in a gleeful way, as some mothers do, she regarded her son as something of a ladykiller, but the aspect of him possibly contracting a disease as a result of his wide and varied behaviour filled her with horror.

'Don't worry mother,' smiled the son, who was all of twenty-two and obviously full of confidence and not only at his prowess as a lover but because as twenty-two year olds often do, he thought he knew EVERY-THING there was to know about life. 'I always carry a bottle of gin with me!'

'Surely there is no need to get them drunk on that?' enquired his mother, somewhat surprised. 'Oh, I don't use it for drinking,' he replied, and to his mother's amazement went on to explain exactly how he used the fluid for disinfecting purposes.

I do hope things continued successfully for the misguided fellow and that he is not, as I suspect, now on a doctor's waiting list.

## S is for JIMMY SAVILE

Once upon a time there was a modest, amiable fellow named Jimmy Savile, who dyed his hair all different, crazy colours to make nasty men think he was a 'fairy' when he worked as a bouncer for Mecca dance halls. This gave them a hell of a shock if they started any trouble but if they were nice, he was nice, and when he came to my Hollywood home on his first visit out there in 1961 he was still very nice.

Then something happened. He bacame a television star which enabled him to buy five Rolls-Royces and loads of big gold rings, bracelets and necklaces. He got an OBE and did lots of work for charity.

Sadly, the Jimmy Savile who had helped me wash the dishes in Hollywood and was then so eager to please, seemed to change completely, to the extent that the last time I saw him he was quite unable to carry on an ordinary conversation, so immersed was he in the image he had created of himself as some sort of little god who could make people's dreams come true (with the aid of the BBC of course).

If only some folk did not believe their own publicity how much happier, and nicer to others, they would really be.

## S is for ARTHUR SCARGILL

Described as 'one of the most notorious Reds under Britain's sagging bedstead', self-styled 'King' Arthur is a very plausible, silver-tongued chap who would have us all thinking that if he really were King, or at the very least Prime Minister, everyone's life would be one long sweet song.

I have appeared with him on three occasions, the last being on the Mike Parkinson Show. He is charming, smooth talking, and almost convincing up to a point; but somehow I cannot help feeling an alarming chill run down the back of my neck when he kisses me Hello.

## S is for SCORPIO

Probably the worst sign of the zodiac, and I should know, for not only am I one myself, but in the past I've had two Scorpio husbands!

Scorpio men are sexy, magnetic and passionate, but they are also jealous, possessive, unreasonable, ruthless and often downright lethal!

There is a saying, 'The devil has a field day when he finds a Scorpio with nothing to do,' and if any woman still doubts my opinion of these men, just recall the war and picture those two generals, Montgomery and Rommel, chasing each other around the desert. They were both Scorpios!

## S is for SCOTSMEN

Do we honestly care any more *what* they have under their kilts? For much too long this tired old question has been trundled out, usually by Scotsmen eager to excite women into thinking they have something better than their English rivals. Frankly, I think that if Billy 'The Big Yin' Connolly is concealing anything that resembles his face, or that ghastly beard, then it's small wonder the only bird who really fancies him is comedienne Pamela Stephenson!

## S is for SEX MANIACS

An evil breed. What angers me more than anything is the way many rapists seem to get off lightly once they are brought to court.

I do not know if it is something appertaining to the permissive society and judges thinking that because most women are liberated when it comes to sex any man can have what he wants from any woman. I've seen cases where rapists have got fifteen or eighteen months in prison which proves that the laws concerning rape are disgraceful.

As for the sex-maniacs who indecently assault young children, God save them from the other inmates if they do get sent to prison by a sensible judge.

## S is for FRANK SINATRA

I have known 'Ole Blue Eyes for over a quarter of a century now (what a terrifying thought) and found him to be a very charming man, totally unlike the image created by the press against whom he has waged a private war throughout his career.

His prowess as a husband and lover I leave to the likes of ex-wives Nancy, Ava Gardner and Mia Farrow to expand upon, but I'm sure a great deal was left to be desired.

However, the lad does have a good sense of humour,

as was proved by a story he once told me about Hitler, when we were both appearing in cabaret at a place called Lake Tahoe in Nevada.

Sinatra is a man of very strong political views, so much so that during Franco's reign as President of Spain he sent a personal letter informing him that he would never return there, because he did not approve of the way Franco ran the country. However, I am deviating, rather in the way that he does, depending whether or not he is a friend of either the Republican or Democrat Presidential candidate when it comes to election time.

Having launched upon an angry tirade about politicians in general, Frank went on to berate other people who did not agree with his own political beliefs, particularly a well-known extreme right-wing group in Hollywood consisting of columnist Hedda Hopper, who literally ran the town in her day, director John Ford and actors John Wayne and Ward Bond, two of Ford's constant screen employees who appeared in almost every film he made.

'Ward Bond,' seethed Sinatra, 'would ride round town on a motor cycle wearing a black shirt, and spouting fascism.'

I smiled inwardly at the thought, for the vision of Bond, who was at the time playing an old wagon master in a television series called *Wagon Train*, looking like an aged Marlon Brando in *The Wild One*, was quite amusing.

'I decided to teach him a lesson,' shouted Sinatra, who by now had worked himself up to a frenzy about the entire matter. He proceeded to relate a story to his captive dinner guests, regarding the time when he visited Germany long after the death of Hitler.

Having found the spot where the Führer was presumed to be buried Sinatra, in his usual way, leaving no holds barred, commissioned a photographer to

162

accompany him there and take his picture. This was however to be no ordinary snapshot of an American tourist gazing at the bunker in awe, but a picture showing Sinatra's own personal feelings about Hitler, Fascism, and the whole situation.

'I unzipped my flies, and had the cameraman take a shot of me pissing over the goddamn bastard!' he proudly announced, amidst much laughter.

'Then what did you do?' I asked, realizing the pay-off had not yet come.

'I got the guy to blow up the picture real large,' he replied jubilantly, 'and I sent it to that Fascist sonofa-bitch Bond, signed . . . Very Truly Yours. Frank.'

## S is for SHORT MEN
Small men have big egos. I cannot elaborate further.

## S is for SYLVESTER STALLONE
I have to say that Sylvester Stallone never turned me on, for the simple reason he always reminded me of a younger, darker Boris Karloff. It was something about the shape of his high forehead and rather twisted facial expression!

This ambitious actor who, loyally supported by his wife, literally starved the first few years he spent in Hollywood, hit the super-stardom bracket he always craved with a block-busting film entitled *Rocky* which, to give him credit, was all his own work.

Sadly, as is the way with many actors after they achieve stardom, Stallone left his wife for a beautiful, young actess named Susan Anton but when the pas-sion wore off he returned home full of remorse. Luckily for him his wife loved him enough to take him back.

To date he has made three *Rocky* films and is no doubt a millionaire, so hopefully he does not mind the fact that a soft-porn video, one he was obviously forced to make for money during his 'starvation' period in Hollywood, is being shown around.

As I stated at the beginning of this piece, he never turned me on, so it was no great disappointment when I watched the supposedly sexy star in various positions throughout this epic, particularly a scene where he capers nude in a dancing circle of nymphettes, to find myself totally unmoved. All I can say is, having observed the *entire* Stallone anatomy in detail, his films should be re-entitled 'Droopy'!

## S is for FREDDIE STARR
Freddie Starr is a true genius and genius is not born every day. What it must be like to be *Mrs* Starr I dare not imagine, but now that Freddie has kicked the drug habit which he fell victim to during his wilder days we can, I am sure, look forward to a feast of entertainment in the future.

## S is for ROD STEWART
The gravel-voiced, gravel-faced pop singer who chooses to be a tax exile in the States only visits this country to see his Scottish team play football. If I was a youngster having to pay a third of my earnings in tax I certainly would buy no more of Mr Stewart's records.

If England is good enough to want to keep coming back to, it's good enough to pay tax in.

## S is for SUPERMAN
If this fellow is really so super . . . how come he wears his underpants outside his trousers?

# T

## T is for JIMMY TARBUCK

Despite what I wrote earlier about comedians being miserable, insecure people, there is always somebody who proves to be the exception, and for me that person is 'Tarbie'.

Not only is he one of the few comics who really make me laugh, he is also (and this is unique in showbusiness) a lovely person, unaffected by his success, genuine and natural.

There must be SOMETHING I can blame him for? Oh yes – he was, quite unconsciously, the inspiration behind me writing this book!

## T is for TAURUS

I like these men on the whole, but then they get off to a good start for Taureans are uncomplicated children who also make the best of playmates.

It is, however, unfortunate that all little boys have to grow up – as a baby, even a gorilla is cute!

## T is for TAXI-DRIVERS

In comparison with New York taxi-drivers British cabbies are much politer and far less pushy. However, this was not the case when a certain titled lady, well-known around the Chelsea circles for her drinking habits (which had, by the way, been the reason her family cast her out without a penny), found herself *en route* home one night, once again without the proverbial penny to pay her taxi fare.

The taxi-driver, quite naturally, became extremely

angry when she told him of her plight, but his fury eased considerably after she invited him in with the invitation to let her work off the bill!

A couple of months later she discovered, to her dismay, that as a result of this method of settling her account she was pregnant. By the time she had had an abortion, the ride cost her a small fortune, for in those days abortions were illegal and very expensive.

The moral of this tale really is that women should always remember that a taxi-driver is capable of taking you for a worse ride than most men!

*T is for TEACHERS*
Something about teachers always daunts me for they make me feel ignorant and rather inferior. I often wonder if they are as pompous with their wives at home as they are in the classroom? As Russell Harty, who was once a teacher, is not married I cannot ask *his* wife. But perhaps, as Nicholas Parsons behaves so much like a teacher on his television show, I should ask Mrs Parson instead!

*T is for DENNIS THATCHER*
I think Dennis is probably a much-maligned man – and is also in the unenviable position of being the most pitied husband in the country, for it cannot be easy to be married to the Prime Minister and to be the butt of so many jokes and ridicule.

Indeed in his own right he is a very wealthy and successful businessman, but he must have a great sense of humour to be married to Mrs Thatcher – and you can take that whichever way you like.

*T is for TERRY THOMAS*
Thomas Terence Hoare Stevens, better known as fright-fully English comedian Terry Thomas, has been a friend of mine for nearly thirty years. I first worked

with him on an early television series of his entitled *How Do You View* which was then his 'catch' phrase. He is also godfather to my second son Gary, and whenever he was making films in Hollywood he would stay at my home in Beverly Hills, and allowed me the same hospitality at his home when I came over to film in England.

Terry would always amuse the members of my staff when they went in with his morning tea. There he would be, sitting up in bed despite the warm California climate, wearing a red flannel nightshirt and little red nightcap with the usual tassel dangling on the end of it. At his home in London he had a shield above the bed, sporting his coat of arms and family motto – the head of a benign-looking cow, and the words 'I will not be cowed' written above it.

Terry liked a drink when he returned tired from the studio, for he found Hollywood really too fast compared with his somewhat slow genteel British way of life. This, and the pressures of work perhaps made him drink more than he should have done sometimes. One night while he was staying at my house in London where I was working, a rather frightening thing happened, due to his consumption of too much champagne!

He had been out to dinner with his agent discussing important business matters, and as the evening went on had obviously drunk more than was good for him. Luckily, the agent was still reasonably sober at the end of the meal, and was able to drive him back to my home, safely depositing him in the drawing-room, before going back to his own house, exhausted by the night's activities. Suddenly he was woken by the urgent ringing of his telephone. It was a terrified Terry crying down the other end for help, and all he could decipher from the garbled chatter were the words, 'Help! I've killed her! Her head's come off.' The agent

167

leapt out of bed in a panic, assuring Terry he would rush over immediately.

With a screech of brakes he pulled up in the driveway and, bursting open the front door, found Terry still sobbing about the severed head and muttering 'I've killed her.'

'Who? Who?' implored the agent desperately. Then to his amazement and relief he saw the 'victim'. It was not, thankfully, a woman but a gold cherub which had been standing in the middle of a round velvet seat holding a bowl of flowers in its hand. Terry had drunkenly fallen over the thing, and amidst the confusion in the darkened room, thought he had really beheaded someone. I was not informed of all this until, upon returning, I noticed a new cherub had been quietly and subtly replaced by my embarrassed house guest.

## T is for TOREADORS
Toreadors, matadors, bull fighters, call them what you like . . . any man who not only makes his living by slaughtering bulls but probably gets a kick out of it too (though not in the right place for my money) is, from a woman's point of view, either very boring or certifiable.

## T is for SPENCER TRACY
Spencer was one of those terrific natural actors. It seemed to come so easily to him – and those films he made with Katherine Hepburn, the love of his life, were super.

However, in those scenes where Spencer had his head bowed and everyone thought were great sensitive moments, are nothing of the sort: He was trying to find his chalk mark on the floor telling him where to stand!

I was lucky enough to be asked out by a producer

friend when he was invited to have dinner with Spencer and some other friends. As is always the way when actors get together, the conversation revolved solely around acting.

Everyone seemed to be disagreeing on the subject – though being young and in the early days of my career, I did not dare venture an opinion. I eventually noticed that Spencer Tracy was particularly silent as well.

The producer, in a desperate attempt to get the great man to join in the conversation, turned to him and said, 'Well, what do you think Spence? What do you think about acting as it is today? Should one adopt the Method or take a different attitude?'

Tracy paused for a moment, as if giving the matter serious thought, then he replied, 'All you gotta do is learn the goddam lines'!

## T is for TRANSVESTITES

Not many people truly understand that if a man is a transvestite, which means he has a fetish about dressing up in women's clothes, it does not necessarily make him a homosexual.

There is nothing desperately wrong if a man wishes to indulge himself in this behaviour, unless of course he is married, as many transvestites are, and does so in front of his children.

I knew one transvestite whose desires were so strong, he spent vast amounts of money on expensive dresses and silk underwear, yet kept his wife and family in poverty.

His wife was a very understanding woman who tried to help him when the urge, which overcame him every so often, really took command of him, but even she could not hide things totally from their children, especially when on summer holidays they noticed that 'Daddy had shaved his legs, unlike other Daddies'.

Not so understanding, or fortunate, was a well-known actress whose husband's transvestite urges became so irresistible that he regularly came down to breakfast dressed as a woman, in front of their three daughters. Needless to say, *that* marriage ended in divorce!

## T is for TURKS
I just hope, for her sake, that if any woman becomes involved with a Turk, he is nothing like those portrayed in the film *Midnight Express*.

## T is for TYCOONS
Shirley Maclaine said it: 'Business-men are too busy making money to fall in love'! Besides which it is not always the ultimate dream when a woman marries one of these men, as the wives of Sir Freddie Laker and John DeLorean might testify, for even the cleverest of them *can* go bust!

If, on the other hand, a tycoon is highly successful and therefore extremely wealthy, a wife may see very little of him, for usually he is so wrapped up in business from early morning till late at night that he leaves a great deal to be desired as a mate.

Lord Grade's wife does not seem to mind her husband's activities, but the urge to make more and more money does take some of them over to the extent that they neglect everything else in the process. A wealthy business friend of mine used to get up each morning at five a.m., work at home for three hours before going to his office, and not return until late at night. His wife, who was also childless, took to gambling to ease the boredom of her life, hoping that when he had made his first million she would see more of him.

Sadly, the urge to achieve his goal gradually obsessed him to the extent that when he actually did it, he resolved to see how long it would take him to

170

make the *second* million, so his wife saw even less of him than before.

Tycoons can also sometimes be tyrannical in their behaviour towards others who have less tenacity than themselves where work is concerned.

A story involving the late tycoon Sir Billy Butlin is related in business circles. It appears that he was making a tour of one of his holiday camps when he came across two men loafing around in dungarees, doing nothing in particular.

Sir Billy was outraged and, waving aside their protestations demanded they go straight to his office. After giving them a good ticking-off, stating that laziness was something he would certainly not tolerate, he demanded their cards in order to dismiss them officially, only then to discover that they were not his employees at all but two campers trying to enjoy their holiday!

*T is for TYRANTS*
I have never known of a tyrant yet who did not eventually wind up on his arse!

# U

*U is for UNFAITHFUL MEN*

Are men more guilty of being unfaithful than women? It can be argued, of course, that if a man wants sex he has to find a woman with whom to have it, but there is also the fact that *she* may not be the one who is married.

Statistically, more married men are unfaithful than women. Man's very nature is that of the hunter, finding excitement in the chase and the conquest, but seeing no more in it than a night's fun.

Perhaps it's their attitude towards the matter that really is the worst part. An actress friend of mine whose husband, a film producer, was at home a great deal between pictures whilst she was out working told me about his antics.

'The trouble started,' she said, 'when I found a pair of knickers in the rubbish bin and when I challenged him about them he said they were perfectly normal things to discover there, and anyway I shouldn't have such a nasty suspicious mind'!

This man was a somewhat unusual type, inasmush as he assumed his wife was going to swallow such a preposterous statement (which, by the way, she did not and they eventually divorced), whereas most men will go to all sorts of lengths to avoid being caught out.

My first husband was a notorious womanizer. As I toiled at the film studio all day, he thoroughly enjoyed himself with as many women as possible. At our last home together we had an indoor swimming-pool, and there, unbeknown to myself, he entertained girls who

splashed around in the water quite happily, besides
doing other things, until a certain time in the afternoon
when he would look at his watch and announce, 'All
right, everybody out.' By the time I arrived home an
hour or so later, the girls had long gone, my bathing
suits were dried, and he would be waiting for me with
a smile, inquiring sympathetically, if I had had a hard
day?

One assistant director with whom I worked on a film
took a fancy to my blonde stand-in, despite the fact he
and his new wife were so consumed with jealousy
about each other, and the possibility that anyone else
might upset their marital bliss, that they argued and
bickered constantly, both accusing the other of all
kinds of imaginary infidelities.

Having just got married, they had acquired a house
which they had not yet moved into but were still
furnishing, and on the fateful night in question the
wife went away to visit her mother.

The husband invited my stand-in out for drinks at
the end of the day's filming, and from there on to his
house where inevitably they wound up in bed together
in, strangely, the guest bedroom.

For reasons of her own, the wife suddenly decided
to arrive home rather unexpectedly (perhaps she had
a suspicion as females often do) and there she discovered her husband and his paramour.

The scene that followed was an ugly one, with the
wife not only physically attacking her mate, but also
scratching, kicking and punching my stand-in and
pulling out great handfuls of her hair.

Needless to say, she did not turn up for work next
day, so bad were her injuries, whilst the truly guilty
party sheepishly attempted to explain what had
occurred using the same idiotic excuse he had tried on
his wife.

'I only invited her back to the house because she had

173

missed the last bus,' he whined, 'and during the night I thought she might be cold in the guest room, so I just went in to see if she was all right.'

My own father, a man who lived rigidly by Victorian principles, was also unfaithful once, to my knowledge, with his secretary.

'Auntie Vi', as I called her, was an unmarried lady who obviously had designs on him, judging by the gifts she bought him (and me too, come to think of it) on birthdays and at Christmas.

One summer evening my mother and I went to the cinema, and on our return saw Auntie Vi's bicycle leaning against the wall of our house. As she had made herself so popular by giving me presents, I rushed excitedly, and a bit too quickly, inside shouting, 'Auntie Vi,' noisily, whilst my mother followed a bit more slowly.

It struck her as odd that the curtains in the back room were drawn, particularly as it was still daylight, and also that the aforementioned 'Aunty' emerged looking shocked and pale with her hair, which she normally wore in a sort of bun, cascading untidily around her shoulders.

Naturally, at nine years old, the significance of the scene escaped me and I listened interestedly as she trundled out an excuse about having arrived at the house and fallen off her bike!

My father, whose policy it was never to tell a lie, even if it meant being dragged to the scaffold, remained strangely silent regarding the affair, not even bothing to go outside and inspect the bicycle for dents, which she made a great show of doing. My mother, however, worked the facts out for herself and later, long after I was in bed, challenged him as to what he had been up to.

Perhaps, because he was my father, I am defending him when I say that at least he made a full honest confession instead of offering a pack of lies as most men would have done.

## U is for UNION MEN

'You can't get me, I'm part of the union.' That's how the song goes. Of course, it was meant to be a bit of fun, but the trouble is most union men do seem to think they are untouchable. They constantly refer to the rule book, spouting off about rule nine, section 148, at the drop of a hat – and also drop everything and stop work as often as they can.

I am not against a fair deal for all, and I would never expect workers to be happy with being misused, but it is the red militant who is out to destroy our society – through the unions – that makes my blood boil.

There can only be one thing worse than working with one of these men, and that's living with him; his wife must expect him home at any odd time, if he has managed to call the firm out on strike, and she often has to put up with heated meetings in her front room. It must be hell, especially if she is not such a political animal as he is. I would not put it past these union men to get the rule book out and have a secret ballot before they can decide whether to have sex or not.

# V

*V is for VALENTINO*
Any woman who saw the film version of the personal
life of this supposedly Great Lover could only have
been bitterly disappointed, as it seems (if we are to
believe the plot) his wife most certainly was!

*V is for VINCENT VAN GOGH*
Was this temperamental painter so misguided and ill-
informed about the female sex that he seriously
thought cutting off his ear and sending it to the woman
who had rejected him, would actually turn her on and
win her back? Well, what else would one expect from
a demented Dutchman!

*V is for VENTRILOQUISTS*
Ventriloquists are strange men, invariably winding up
mad, or, at the very least genuinely thinking the doll
they manipulate is real.
   A girl friend of mine once had a romance with a
famous ventriloquist. One of the tasks he gave her was
to hand the wooden dummy through the curtain to
him on stage when he was ready. The affair floundered
eventually, or perhaps I should say inevitably, for any
man who spends most of his time with his hand up a
puppet's arse must leave a great deal to be desired
when it comes to anything else!

## V is for VICARS

I can sympathize (I think) and find it in my heart to forgive the odd vicar who, through inescapable circumstances, falls in love with someone else's wife and runs off with her, thereby creating an appalling scandal and a bad reputation for religion and for the church by doing so.

But 'GAY' Vicars? These are a group now formed in this new permissive society of ours ... NEVER, NEVER, NEVER!

## V is for VILLAINS

Let me say right away that I do not condone things any criminal has ever done against the law. But sometimes I think that same law inflicts sentences that are unreasonable on the wrong people.

The Kray twins went to prison for life and without them London is no longer a safe place to be. For as I have always maintained the Krays did not mug old ladies or batter little children. They confined their gruesome activities to other gangsters within their own empire.

Criminals whom I felt also received overlong sentences were the Great Train Robbers. I know what they did was wrong, but compared with some of the terrible crimes committed since, I think thirty years for robbing a train was unfair.

It was while serving his own massive sentence that one of the Train Gang, Tommy Wisbey, learned about the tragic death of his daughter. She was killed in a road accident.

The Home Office refused to let Tommy out – even under guard – to attend the funeral. I thought that was inhumane and I sent Tommy a telegram of sympathy. He wrote back and a little flurry of letters passed between us.

One day he sent my son Jason a beautiful teddy bear,

fully dressed, and had been hand made by one of his fellow inmates. Naturally, I sent Tommy a 'thank-you' letter and he replied he was glad I had received the present because he had sent it some weeks earlier and he was worried if it had gone astray.

'Trains do sometimes get hijacked you know,' he wrote mischievously. Villains, rogues, scoundrels or rascals, whichever one prefers to call them, they do seem to have an irresistible attraction for many women, including a friend of mine who was hopelessly in love with an American gangster. We were at his plush apartment in New York one night having a few drinks when the gangster, a little worse for booze, started boasting about his life of crime.

Drunkenly swaggering into the kitchen he flung open the door of a huge fridge and pointed to a rather large chicken reclining on one of the shelves.

'Stick your hand up its arse,' yelled our host. We all looked at each other, none of us quite willing to do what he said indeed, mystified by his strange demand.

'Stick your hand up its arse,' he yelled again, but louder. By this time we were a little afraid that he might pull a revolver from somewhere, so one brave soul, actor Jess Conrad put his hand up the chicken's posterior . . . only to reveal the gangster's latest haul . . . $100,000 in dollar bills!

*V is for VIRGO*

Virgo men start being difficult as children, when they criticize everything and anything their parents do.

They are fastidious about cleanliness, which is not a bad fault, but because of this hang-up they also find it very hard to being themselves to kiss a member of the opposite sex without thinking of all the germs she might be passing on.

This, of course, does not encourage much passion in a woman, neither does straightening all the cushions on the sofa before a love-making session. By the time Mr Virgo has the scene set to his satisfaction, the lady could well have changed her mind about what she saw in him in the first place.

*V is for VOYEURS*
These sick men are almost as bad as 'gay' vicars, but at least they have the decency to keep their behaviour private, locked away in the closet or wherever they choose to hide the spyholes they use to watch others doing things they are incapable of themselves.

# W

*W is for MAX WALL*

Timing is everything in life! This brilliant comedian's great mistake was being born when there was no such thing as the permissive society, and if men were unfaithful to their wives they did not do it blatantly.

Having been married for some years to a good woman who bore his five children, Max fell in love with a young beauty queen and left home for her.

The public were so outraged by his behaviour that his career was destroyed totally, to the extent that he was booed off the stage and even spat at in certain places when he endeavoured to perform his comedy act.

Times change (except maybe in Wales) and gradually broken marriages and men and women just living together, were no longer frowned upon my society in the old Victorian way. After twenty years or so Max Wall was finally forgiven for his actions, though *never* by his children, and allowed to continue entertaining audiences with his marvellous talents.

Perhaps I should have written this piece under W for Womanizing, as even after the marriage with the beauty queen floundered Max still never learnt a lesson and proceeded to be hurt by various other women, again and again. 'I will never change,' he confessed to me once. 'I love women too much, in fact I worship them! The only thing is, nowadays, all I really want is someone who will put a blanket over me if I'm cold.'

I suppose the moral of this sad little tale is that if he had stayed with his wife, instead of chasing other women, she would be doing just that for him, whilst they sat happily surrounded by their grandchildren.

## W is for WELSHMEN

At the risk of hundreds of Welsh wives, including relatives of mine, rising in uproar against me, I have to say that I think Welshmen win first prize for male chauvinism.

In the bad old days when women HAD to sit at home whilst their husbands went out and did whatever they liked, Welsh wives were subservient and dutifully catered to their menfolk without complaint. However, today whilst others have gone beyond this state of affairs, many Welshmen still treat their women in the same manner their fathers and grandfathers did.

Give a Welshman the chance of a romantic evening with his wife – over a candle-lit dinner perhaps? – or an evening at the pub, drinking beer, playing darts and telling rugby stories, with the boys, they will opt for the latter every time, regardless of what the 'little woman at home' thinks!

## W is for WIGWEARERS

Call them toupées, rugs, or whatever you like, but when a man sticks a bit of artificial hair on the top of his bald pate, he is wearing a wig and thus displaying the fact that he is also extremely vain!

I have written about Bruce Forsyth twice in this book, so it would be unfair to discuss the new idiotic thatch which perches on top of his head. Everyone else has already made fun of it, anyway!

It is, of course, common knowledge that Sean Connery, whom I like tremendously because he is a down-to-earth human being, wears a wig when acting on screen, but it is precisely because he is honest and earthy that he would never dream of sporting the thing in private life.

Reginald Bousanquet is another matter!

Also a sex symbol, in his own odd way when reading the ten o'clock news, Reggie stirred women's fantasies and excited them at the end of a tiring day.

The thought that he might have to leave half his head on a wooden block beside the bed they imagined sharing with him, made not a scrap of difference in their minds for after all, up there on the television screen he was as unreal as his artificial mop. How disillusioned some of his female fans must have been, however, when Reggie once opened a fête on a summer afternoon. Unfortunately, as is often the way with an English summer the weather was not very good, in fact it was downright windy, and whilst performing the opening ceremony, a blustering gust fetched his wig straight off. Happily, a gentleman nearby came to the rescue . . . by reaching up and spearing the stupid thing with his shooting stick!

## W is for SIR HAROLD WILSON

Firstly, let me point out that I have no interest in politics, or, for that matter, politicians, other than as part of my research into men.

Sir Winston Churchill was a great Prime Minister and I will not dwell on him as I have already 'done' him under the letter C, except to say that actor Richard Burton once chose to make some very scathing statements about the old boy whilst portraying him in a TV play.

Every public figure is open to criticism and comment, but Richard's remarks were extremely distasteful, particularly as Sir Winston had passed on. However, he received his 'come-uppance' for doing this soon after in the shape of a riddle about him which went round: 'Why was Richard Burton's father the greatest carpenter in Wales? Because, with just one screw, he made the biggest shit-house in the country.'

But back to Sir Harold Wilson.

I was not a staunch supporter of his during the three terms of office he enjoyed, unlike a good many of my show-business contemporaries, but it was stupid of me not climb on to the Wilson bandwagon when it was rolling, as many others did, for now I might be the proud possessor of a decoration such as the M.B.E., C.B.E. or O.B.E.

I am all for people being knighted, recognized and thanked for services rendered to the public, and general welfare of humanity, but to bestow honours upon actors is a joke in my opinion, for really they have done nothing much except make a living in a fairly easy racket, as film star Robert Mitchum so aptly describes show-business!

In the old days when decorations truly meant something, it was an honour, but not today. When the late John Lennon sent his MBE for being a Beatle back, I was the first to applaud his courageous convictions.

During Harold Wilson's reign as Prime Minister, when he was aided by the domineering Lady Falkender (note they bestowed titles on themselves, despite the fact that as Socialists everyone is supposed to be on the same level) many show-business folk were awarded decorations. Apart from Lady 'Forkbender's' obsession with the theatre, there was also an actor who became great friends with Harold himself, to such an extent that he would spend weekends at Chequers advising him on certain matters, and keeping him laughing as in the old days of the Court Jesters with the King.

It was he who helped start the much-publicized and criticized cocktail parties at Number 10. These became such an everyday occurrence, with show-business people dropping in at odd times for drinks, that newspapers began commenting and lampooning the situation so much that things had to be calmed down.

Whilst all this partying and merrymaking was going on, actors, actresses, disc-jockeys and singers were having MBEs and OBEs dished out for their 'services to show-business' like jellybeans, thus making a mockery of something which had once been a distinction of honour and respect.

One actor, before being actually knighted, declared publicly that 'anyone who was not a Socialist was not worth knowing, and merited nothing'. He then commenced to sell his house at an enormous profit, but never shared the proceeds with his political party, or even donated some of it to charity, which presumably is what Socialism is all about!

When I look back on the Wilson regime now and read revelations of the 'goings on' at Number 10, the titles bestowed upon all and sundry, and the sudden decision to retire taken by Sir Harold at a disastrous moment in our history, it gives me terrible forebodings about politics and the men who run our country – Mrs Thatcher excluded of course!

*W is for TERRY WOGAN*
I adore Terry Wogan. He is a nice looking, intelligent, and humorous man, in fact the kind you want to take home to meet your mother. She would adore him . . . and your father would like him too!

He is, I'll bet, a wonderful husband, and a marvellous parent to his children. All in all the *perfect* man!

But then I have to remember there is no such person, so what could be wrong with Wogan? He must do something bad when he gets home, like kicking the cat, or swearing at his wife. I WISH I knew what it was!

*W is for WRESTLERS*
I know the sight of a man with rippling muscles often turns a woman on, but how any of them can be fooled by these 'all-in wrestlers' is beyond me.

When I was very young, and knew not a lot, I used to think such men were goliaths, strong and downright dangerous to tangle with, particularly in the ring. But then I discovered that wrestling is all nonsense and, unlike in boxing which is a genuine sport, these wrestling men are simply putting on an act.

Oh well, yet another illusion shattered!

## W is for WRITERS

I have always had a soft spot for writers, probably because the majority I have met are highly intelligent men, often with a quick wit, and good sense of humour.

To be *married* to a writer, however, must be a very different thing, and whilst all of them are obviously not the same I will take several just to partially prove my point.

The greatest one, William Shakespeare, left much to be desired as a husband, it appears. Although his wife, Anne Hathaway, has been described as a nagger, perhaps she had good cause; Will was never at home penning his brilliant works, nor was she the woman to whom he composed his beautiful love sonnets.

Eugene O'Neill, the American writer, had many tempestuous relationships with women and several marriages, the last being the strangest one of all. Even when his wife was very ill and he lay dying, they were still fighting so intensely that their friends could not mention to either one that the other was in hospital.

Two more American writers, Ernest Hemingway and Scott Fitzgerald, the latter being a chronic alcoholic, experienced disastrous love lives and marriages as dramatic as their novels, many of which later became known to an even wider audience when they were made into films.

Finally there is our own Harold Pinter who left his wife, actress Vivian Merchant, so utterly miserable when he left her and married Lady Antonia Fraser, that she died soon after of a broken heart combined with the effects of heavy drinking.

# X

*X is for MR X*
As opposed to Madame X, usually the lady in a divorce suit not wishing to be named, there are plenty of *Mr X*'s creeping in and out of lady's bedchambers who are never discovered and thus do not have to appear in court at all.

The most notorious one I ever knew was quite unique in as much as, unlike millions of other men who do not get on with their mothers-in-law this one got on top of his, regularly.

Of course, there was an ulterior reason for his disgraceful love-making sessions, which took place several times a year . . . the lady was extremely rich, and always rewarded him with an expensive present for services rendered but thankfully none of their exploits were known to his wife and children.

*X is for FATHER XMAS*
This jolly and generous gentleman must be the PER-FECT man, BUT sadly he does not exist!

Also interesting is the fact that even in fantasy, once again the male of the species gets the credit, for after the business of catering to his needs all year whilst he prepares toys for the festive season poor 'Mother Xmas' never even rates a mention!

# Y

*Y is for JESS YATES*

To parody the saying, 'Hell hath no fury like a man scorned!': not many people realize that the downfall of the television Bishop, Jess Yates, was initiated by Hughie Green after they had had an almighty row.

After the argument, Hughie used all his power and contacts to spill the beans about the 'Bishop' and his fancy woman.

It ruined Jess of course. He could no longer go on presenting a religious programme when the whole country knew he was married and having an affair.

If only he had made it known that he was separated from his wife and had a girlfriend, there might not have been quite the uproar that ensued when he was subsequently 'de-frocked' by a newspaper.

Frankly, I had no sympathy for the man as I had once told my agent that I was interested in doing a *Stars on Sunday* but the message came back through a minion that there was no way would they have me on the show with my tempestuous publicity background.

The Bishop also refused to have Diana Rigg on his show, even though her early publicity had been nowhere near as bad as mine. Diana's 'crime' was that she was living with a man who was not her husband.

I frequently used to get irate whenever I tuned in and saw who was actually on his show. I knew some of the 'butter wouldn't melt in their mouths' starlets had actually been personally vetted by Jess himself.

Perhaps if this actress had gone to bed with the Bishop I may have made the show too!

187

## Y is for YES MEN

American superstars seem to make a habit of having 'Yes' men around them all the time. 'Yes' men are the sort of people I cannot stand.

If they were women I wouldn't be able to stand them either, but as they are invariably men, and that is who I am writing about in this book, then it is them I must discuss.

My first experience of real one hundred per cent yes men was when I was once asked to appear with Bob Hope on his own television spectacular which he was filming over here in England.

I was summoned to the Dorchester HOtel where he was staying, ushered up to the fabulous suite he had taken over, and introduced to Bob Hope for the first time.

To my amazement he was surrounded by eighteen men all of whom, I found out, were his writers and on his pay-roll. It was like something out of the days of the court of Henry VIII.

Every time Bob opened his mouth to make a joke, whether it was vaguely funny or not, all these men would burst into uncontrollable laughter. But if Bob looked glum, they looked glum.

'Yes' men are not the type of men I could ever admire or respect and can also be found in any big business concern.

## Y is for the YORKSHIRE RIPPER

Few men can have struck such terror into women's souls than the Yorkshire Ripper did during the years the police were vainly trying to discover who he was.

The thought of a strange man lurking in dark alleys and springing out wielding a hammer was terrifying, particularly as the original Jack the Ripper's identity was never revealed back in the 1890s because he was not caught.

Unlike the modern-day ripper, Peter Sutcliffe, whose plea of schizophrenia failed and who was put behind bars for life, the Victorian ripper remains a sinister mystery to this day. There have been many theories as to who he was, some of which include a frustrated homosexual with a hatred for women and a doctor whose prowess with a knife was quite remarkable. But the silliest rumour, perhaps started by the Ripper himself, was that it could be a WOMAN, which is something I will never believe!

### Y is for YOUNG HUSBANDS

Age doesn't matter a damn when you are in love and when you think you can make marriage a success. People seem to be obsessed with the belief that marriages between couples of wildly different ages or where the wife is older can never work.

Well, they do. Alan is nine years younger than me and we have been married for fifteen years at the time of writing this book. HOwever, I hasten to say it has to be worked at, whatever your age gap may be.

### Y is for YOUNG MEN

Young men deliver what old men can only promise or, as the French say, 'Si la jeunesse savait, si la vieillesse pauvait'.

### Y is YUL BRYNNER

Strictly speaking he should be under B but who could resist putting him under Y? (I'm short of Y's anyway.)

Indeed, what woman could resist the bald-headed Yul? At least I'm sure that is what he thought when he first had the brilliant idea of shaving his head smooth as a billiard ball, which he knew women could not help but want to caress.

If in his early acting days Yul had not come up with such a brainwave, he may by now have been among

189

the masses of unforgettable male stars who have blazed a short trail and disappeared from our screens, for certainly he is no great actor in the Laurence Olivier class, even when posturing in yet another version of *The King and I*.

However, I am willing to bet 'Mrs Yul's' feelings about having a bald husband were never considered!

### Y is for YUGOSLAVIANS

The only Yugoslavian I knew was one of the most beautiful men I have ever seen. He made Warren Beatty look like the Hunchback of Notre Dame – but oh those Slavic moods!

The intensity of how a Yugoslavian feels when he is in love can only be described as lethal, so the warning for any woman who becomes heavily involved emotionally is, BEWARE! It was a sullen Slav who shot Mickey Rooney's ex-wife Barbara during a love affair they were having and then turned the gun on himself.

# Z

*Z is for Zoologists*

I was 13 and living at home in Swindon when I fell for the tall dark schoolboy whose mother had a beautiful house with a private lake on which we used to go boating on sunny summer afternoons.

Neither of us could ever have dreamt then what would become of us. I went on to be Britain's number one sex symbol and he became Dr Desmond Morris, author of *The Naked Ape*. I just hope I was not part of his inspiration!

*Z is for THE END OF THE BOOK!*

As the letter Z comes at the end of the alphabet, and this is the end of the book, I would just like to say that I trust the man in YOUR life is nothing like the descriptions I have given within these pages, be they signs of the Zodiac or anything else.

If I have been accurate then it will, I hope, serve as a help to you in both the present and the future, for the past is finished and if you have had, or still have, a man in your life who is at all like anyone I have written about, at least you will know what to do with him!

However, at the opposite end of the scale, if this book did not come close to describing any man you know, or have ever known, then you are indeed blessed.

I suppose as a last gesture, for I have not been too kind to men whilst penning my observances or opinions, I must concede the fact that not only do I love them, but it would certainly be a dull, old world without them!

*M is for MEN*
I know this is just a scene from a Hollywood movie I once made, but somehow it depicts the sort of men by whom I have been surrounded all my life, namely a priest, a lawyer, a police chief and a judge! They always looked miserable and consequently made me look miserable too.